UA Training Technologies: 5

Using Case Studies, Simulations, and Games in Human Resource Development

Using Case Studies, Simulations, and Games in Human Resource Development

J. William Pfeiffer, Ph.D., J.D.

Arlette C. Ballew

University Associates, Inc.
8517 Production Avenue
San Diego, California 92121

Table of Contents

Introduction 1

1. A Background for Using Case Studies in
Human Resource Development 3
    Definition 3
    The History of the Case-Study Method 4
    What a Case Study Is 5
    What a Case Study Is Not 6
    A Rationale for Using Case Studies 6
    The Purpose of Using Case Studies 8

2. Using Case Studies 11
    Selecting a Case Study 11
    Preparation 14
    Presenting a Case Study 15
    Case Studies in Program Development 21
    Sources of Cases 22

3. Developing Case Studies 25
    To Write or To Buy 25
    Research 26
    Writing 33
    Notes for the Facilitator 39
    Revising 40
    Getting the Release 42

4. A Background for Using Simulations in
Human Resource Development 45
    What a Simulation Is and What It Is Not 45
    A Rationale for Using Simulations 48
    The History of Simulations 50

5. Developing Simulations 53
   Understanding Aspects of Simulations 53
   Stages in Developing a Simulation 55
   Random Numbers, Stochastic Variables, and the
      Monte Carlo Method 59
   The Decision Tree 61
   The Difference Between Simulations and Games . . . 62

6. A Background for Using Games in Human
   Resource Development 65
   What Simulation Games Are 65
   A Rationale for Using Games 68
   The History of Simulation Games 69
   Game Structures and Types of Games 73

7. Evaluating and Selecting Games 79
   A Check List for Evaluating Simulation Games 80
   Staffing Considerations 81

8. Facilitating Games 83
   Prework 83
   Introducing the Game 84
   Conducting the Game 85
   Discussion and Processing 89
   An Example of Group Dynamics in Simulation
      Gaming 90
   Using Simulations to Teach Strategic Planning 92

9. Considerations in Developing Simulation Games 95
   Purpose and Use 95
   The Simulation Model 96
   Stylistic and Functional Issues 97
   Constructing and Testing the Game:
      Time and Money 99

References and Bibliography 103

Appendix 1: An Article on Using Simulation Games 107

Appendix 2: Additional Resources for Simulation Games . . . 123

Introduction

The purpose of experiential training is to let participants feel the learning as well as think it, to let them "try on" new behaviors and new emotional as well as cognitive responses. There are numerous ways to achieve this, and we have discussed many of them in the previous four books in this Training Technologies set: *Using Structured Experiences in Human Resource Development; Using Instruments in Human Resource Development; Using Lecturettes, Theory, and Models in Human Resource Development;* and *Using Role Plays in Human Resource Development.* All these technologies have been used and refined for decades and they are still the mainstays of much group work. The subjects of this book, case studies, simulations, and games, also have long been part of the trainer's repertoire. But now there is a new kid on the block, the digital computer, and we are seeing some differences in how training is created and conducted. Although most case studies still are presented in written form, some have been "computerized"; even more simulations and games have been transferred to computer technology.

This book attempts to bridge the span between the traditional training methods—in which the participants respond to the facilitator and to physical and written materials—and the new technologies—in which the participants respond to a computer terminal with occasional assistance from the facilitator. As you will see as you read this book, the trainer's role is still crucial. Even with computerized programs, the professional trainer must select the training device to be used, introduce it and tie it to other aspects of the training experience, facilitate the process, keep the human dynamics and interactions moving smoothly, and conduct the processing discussions on which much of the transfer of learning depends. We cannot, however, ignore the fact that trainers increasingly will be called on to use more computerized training programs. Although this book will by no means deal exclusively with this subject—or attempt to turn a trainer into a computer programmer— it will try to explain some of the basic considerations involved in the design and operation of computer simulations and games, in order to help HRD professional to more effectively select and plan training programs that include them. We hope that the discussions that follow will help you to be more effective in selecting and facilitating both traditional and computerized training programs.

1

A Background for Using Case Studies in Human Resource Development

Definition

A case is a description of an administrative decision or problem that people are trying to solve (or a record of an issue that actually has been faced by the people involved, e.g., managers, executives, doctors, engineers, accountants), together with the surrounding circumstances, facts, opinions, and prejudices on which executive decisions depended. It usually is written from the point of view of the decision maker. The case method is the use of cases as educational tools to provide participants an opportunity to put themselves in the decision maker's or problem solver's shoes. The written case is presented to participants or students for exploration, analysis, discussion, and decision about the action to be taken. Through repeated personal analysis, discussion with others, definition of the problem, identification of alternatives, statement of objectives and discussion criteria, choice of action, identification of possible consequences, and plan for implementation, the participants have the opportunity to develop analytical and planning skills (Leenders & Erskine, 1973). The case method includes the case materials and specific ways of using those materials. It also provides the participants with *feedback* on their answers, analyses, recommendations, and decisions.

The History of the Case-Study Method

The case-study method has been used since the early 1900s at the Harvard Business School, which also trained faculty members from other schools in the case method from 1955 to 1965 through a Visiting Professors Case Method Program sponsored by the Graduate School of Business Administration and the Ford Foundation. The Harvard Business School was a leader both in using and in developing case studies for teaching and training, aided by financial and other support from the Ford Foundation. Originally, most of the cases were used in planned organizational change. Action research served as the source of the cases. Cases also were used as examples and as alternatives to "war stories." According to Towl (1969), "The use of cases permitted the professor to convert a subject from static pigeon holes into which pieces of life are put, to an organic system of concepts which can be used to see life more clearly and as a whole."

During the period of time in which the Harvard program was in operation, two studies of academic management education (Pierson et al., 1959; Gordon & Howell, 1959) emphasized the need to teach managers how to make decisions and solve problems, rather than teaching them business "practices" or "techniques." Both studies recommended that the case method be used more. As a result, the faculty members at many colleges and universities began to want to learn how to use the case method.

Initially, at Harvard and other universities, most case studies were used in management training. Although they still primarily are geared to managers and other professionals, case studies now are used in human resource development, management and leadership development, other social sciences, engineering, medicine (including nursing), economics, and many other fields. There are some differences in how case studies are written in various fields. For example, in the legal profession cases are based on precedent, on getting the judge's or jury's decision, not on what the lawyer does. Medical cases usually are based on clinical diagnosis and treatment. Cases in business administration tend to focus on analysis, objectives, and action needed now. This book will discuss the latter type of cases: those intended for use in human resource development, including management training.

What a Case Study Is

In a very general sense, there are four types of cases (Willings, 1968): (a) individual problem, (b) isolated incident, (c) organizational problems, and (d) a combination of some of these. The focus of a case study can be on a person, incident, or situation. Because it is to be used for diagnostic purposes, a written case contains all relevant data about the situation. It does not contain prescriptive data (solutions and the effects of solutions) because these are generated by the participants in the training. The case presents actual events that have occurred in an organization (business, hospital, etc.), covering a variety of human aspects of management (Tagiuri, Lawrence, Barnett, & Dunphy, 1968), to demonstrate the complexity of real-life situations. The case writer includes aspects of the case that are relevant to the training objectives, including economic, technical, social, and personal factors.

Malcolm P. McNair (Towl, 1969), says that the case study:

- has a specific time frame, is written in the past tense, and specifies a sequence of events;
- has a narrative structure—the flow of a story—along with expository structures to explain the context and details to the participants (company, industry, technical, etc.);
- has a plot structure—an issue (what should be/have been done?).

Willings (1969) says that the case-study *process* includes the following: a stated problem and existing information (the written case), needed information, the actual problem, objectives in solving the problem, possible solutions, possible effects of them, best action(s), and ways to deal with the effects and prevent problems in the future.

A good case reaches a balance between facts and people and their feelings. It tells how the situation developed and how it was handled up to the decision point. It bridges the gap between the business or professional setting, with its unique circumstances, jargon, and so on, and the learning group. The facilitator supplies theoretical tools for the participants to use. The participants' task is to *apply* the theories they have learned to the circumstances in the case, decide what is pertinent, identify the real issues, decide what should be done, and develop a plan of action.

What a Case Study Is Not

A case study is not an example, illustration, or demonstration. In actuality, it is more like a mystery story. The case writer does not include his or her own opinions, analysis, evaluation, or answers. This is the domain of the participants, in their private and group work and discussion. Thus, the case study is not used to prove a point, but to develop critical analysis and decision-making skills.

How Case Studies Differ from Games

Case studies are different from learning games. In games, team members actually make decisions and must experience the consequences of them. Rather than analyzing and discussing the situation, as in a case study, the participants in a game become part of it, making a series of decisions and actions over the course of the game. There is more competition and team feeling (and usually, therefore, more pressure). There also may be less consultation, thus, fewer points of view in regard to decisions. Because games have rules, there is less flexibility in how they are presented. A different way of assimilating knowledge, cases are used to *communicate* concepts rather than to *illustrate* them.

A Rationale for Using Case Studies

More and more managers and other professionals are called on to *decide* what to do in a problem situation rather than to follow a prescribed routine. In our "information society" we do not have the time or opportunity to gather or check all the information we need; thus, we rely increasingly on information provided by others. Although we do not have the luxury of checking all the information we receive (that would be inefficient), we must evaluate its implications and possible consequences. In many situations, we cannot even get all the information we would like. At some point, we must decide what is sufficient information on which to base a decision or on which to act. Unfortunately, because organizations and organizational issues today are so complex, we cannot devise a set of answers for "typical" management problems. There are too many complex factors, too many diverse responsiblities. Furthermore, the process of mentoring is no longer common in most organizations. Thus, there is no easy way for the new manager or professional to obtain the benefit of experience.

The case method makes use of past experience as a frame of reference. Written cases allow the process of learning from actual situations, actions, and consequences. A good case is a vehicle by which a piece of reality is brought into the training setting. The case demonstrates the significant aspects of a situation and helps the participants to identify alternatives. The real nature of the case also helps to keep the discussion grounded on some of the facts that must be faced in real-life situations, avoiding the speculation that may arise in purely theoretical learning. In the case method, complex situations must be pulled apart and put together again before they can be understood. This brings out the participants' assumptions, preferences, attitudes, theories, and ways of operating. Participants can look at what their reactions and responses are and compare them with those of others. In this way, and with the input of the group facilitator, they can see factors that they may not have thought of or that might be getting in the way of effectiveness. Thus, they gain new awareness, new insights, new concepts and increased understanding of old ones, in addition to new skills.

Dr. Nathaniel Cantor (Towl, 1969) urged professors in the Harvard Business School program to shift from "teaching" to fostering the conditions for "learning." Associate Dean Lombard of the Harvard Business School said, "The proper role of theory is to direct inquiry" (Towl, 1969). The case-study method does just that; it allows the application of theory to practice. The learning that occurs is much more likely to be used than is rote memorization.

In addition, the case method may be one of the few available training technologies that would be tolerated by people who have advanced knowledge or understanding. Teachers, lawyers, doctors, managers, and others who have had years of experience may be amenable to exploring ideas with a group about how to deal with complex problems, whereas they may not be inclined to sit and listen to a lecture or presentation that reminds them of a conventional classroom.

The Purpose of Using Case Studies

In today's world, most professional and managerial jobs consist of a series of decisions involving the weighing of alternatives in the context of managing the inevitable change. Young professionals generally have knowledge in their specialized fields, but not in management processes. One purpose of the case-study method is to acquaint the participants with a range of actual professional or management situations that require decisions and action.

A second goal is to allow them to relate these situations to relevant theory, models, and knowledge. As old methods become obsolete, they need to learn how to absorb, interpret, and use new relationships and new knowledge. To achieve this, learning must be realistic and useful. In this regard, the participants are not actually trying to learn information or a specific body of knowledge from the case, but to *practice using* the information or knowledge in making critical distinctions in a variety of situations.

This leads us to the most important goal of the case-study method: to develop the participant's ability to think, decide, and choose appropriate courses of action. The use of case studies gives the participants experience (and allows them to develop skill) in working with data, relating facts to action, deciding what should be done, and committing to a course of action. Skill takes more time to develop than does intellectual comprehension. Developing problem-solving and decision-making skills helps the participants to deal with the multitude of situations in their professional lives that require action and change. The method teaches them how to think on their feet, quickly and effectively, rather than how to enforce or carry out a static policy.

Lastly, a goal of the case-study method is to get the participants *involved,* so that they understand the need to engage in the process and take responsibility for both the outcome and their own learning (i.e., content and process). With involvement and experience, they also gain confidence in using their new skills.

2

Using Case Studies

Selecting a Case Study

In designing a training program, the facilitator first needs to identify both the objectives of the training program and the skill levels
of the participants and then select theoretical materials and experiential technologies that will best meet these objectives and the
needs of the training group. There are many experiential
technologies available, including instruments, structured experiences, role plays, case studies, simulations, and games. All can
be used to create an interaction between the theories, models, and
concepts presented and the realities of everyday life. In considering the goals of the training and the conceptual input to be
presented, the facilitator must decide what balance there will be
between cognitive input and experiential learning. Then, with a
complementary balance in mind, the facilitator can decide how this
will be achieved. Will the cognitive input consist of lectures,
readings, lecturettes, handouts, and/or audiovisual aids? Which experiential technologies will work best? There are various effects
of each alternative, and these must be considered carefully. Above
all, the facilitator should not choose to use a structured experience,
role play, or case study simply because he or she likes to do it. The
case study is an effective way to illustrate concepts and reinforce
theory. It also presents and allows for various points of view. If the
facilitator's objective is to help the participants to use concepts to
analyze situations and make decisions, the case study may be the
best alternative.

Relating the Case Study to Learning Goals

If the facilitator decides that the use of a case study is appropriate, the next task is to find one that raises the issues the facilitator wants to deal with. The facilitator must select a case that can be completed adequately within the time available. Many of the case studies written for human resource development take from three to six hours, and some cases take longer. A case study should be *involving*, but it is not intended to be "entertaining"; completing it is work. Thus, any case to be used with a learning group should be interesting, so that it will involve the participants, but the primary question in selecting a case is whether it will teach the things that need to be taught. The issue or problem in the case study must be relevant to the rest of the training program. The facilitator must ask: "What are the goals *of* and *for* the participants?" At the end of this chapter there is a discussion of sources of written case studies; many are available from libraries or other standard HRD sources. It may take a lengthy search to find a case study that is exactly right; however, it is better not to use a case study than to use an inappropriate one.

Technological Considerations

Some case studies now are available on computer disk. Each participant (or each team of participants) obtains and processes data at a computer terminal. On some programs, the participants can alter numerical data (such as sales figures, inventory, salaries, etc.) to explore alternatives.

The computer and other forms of technology have altered the use of the case study in other ways. A new problem in using this technology is the changing role of the computer in finding and analyzing information in today's organizations. In addition, cases are more complex, in part because organizations and economics are more complex. Cases that are a few years old may not reflect these changes or the changes that result from the impact of the many other forms of rapidly changing technology in the "real world." It may be difficult to keep up-to-date on these changes in organizational case studies. This creates the question of obsolesence, the need to keep finding new, up-to-date cases. Some people choose merely to update good, existing cases. Others believe that this is not enough to create a sense of reality for the participants because the *issues* are outdated, and that it is very important that the issues be relevant.

Relating the Case Study to the Participant Group

The case to be used must relate to the type of jobs and level of experience and/or knowledge of the participants. Although case studies are used in college settings as training for future roles, the case-study method primarily is designed to be used with people who can make decisions or take actions in their own organizations or who have authority or responsibility. The participants must be at a level where they can identify with the person (administrator, boss, consultant, etc.) in the case and with that person's job responsibilities. They need to be able to understand the organizational background and situation and the interrelationships in the case as well as the "facts" before they can use the case study effectively. Therefore, they may need some prior knowledge of certain concepts and business practices and some experience to relate to what they are reading in the written case (even though further theoretical input will be given) and as a basis for later analysis and discussion. For this reason, the facilitator must be careful not to select a case that requires a decision that is above the participants' levels of responsibility and understanding.

The facilitator also should be familiar enough with the participants' backgrounds to know where they are likely to go in terms of their analyses and discussion. If participants do not "catch on" to a case, they will criticize it rather than acknowledge their lack of understanding. If this occurs, the fault lies with the facilitator for selecting a case that is inappropriate for the group or for using a case study at all.

It is a good idea for the facilitator to find out what type of organization the participants work for in terms of structure, hierarchy, norms, values, and processes (the ways in which things are done and how they feel). The more closely the case study can relate to them, the more likely it is that the participants will take it seriously and become involved. It is even better if the facilitator can learn what the participants' primary job responsibilities are and what types of decisions they typically make. This may be possible when one is doing in-house training and in some consulting work. It usually is not as possible in public training or in a university or college setting. Of course, it is easier for the facilitator if all the participants are from the same organization or at least have the same educational or professional background. It also is helpful if the geographical location of the organization in the case-study is similar to that of the participants.

Preparation

The facilitator must have a thorough knowledge and understanding of the subject of the case (e.g., management) before attempting to teach it. The facilitator must study the case itself before the training session, even if it is one that he or she has used before. Because a case study is different with each group, the facilitator must be thoroughly familiar with not only the case but also its ramifications, i.e., where the discussion is likely to go, and must prepare for alternatives in terms of the group analysis, discussion, questions, and suggested courses of action. The facilitator may find that he or she varies the case presentation depending on how it worked with the previous group. He or she also must be prepared to deal with the unexpected in presenting and discussing the case. This is a good time to review and add to the facilitator's notes at the end of the case.

Willings (1968) suggests that facilitators ask themselves specific questions when preparing to use a case study. These include:

1. What is likely to be generated by this case?
2. What is the presenting problem? The real problem(s)?
3. Does the facilitator have any biases?
4. What parts of the written case help in identifying and understanding the real problem?
5. How would the facilitator solve it?

6. What questions are the participants likely to ask?

7. Are there any red herrings?

8. How long will various steps in the process take?

The facilitator also must plan where and how to make conceptual inputs. A good source of information in this regard is *Using Lecturettes, Theory, and Models in Human Resource Development,* the third book in this University Associates Training Technologies collection.

The participants in the training group should have an opportunity to become acquainted with one another *before* the case study is introduced so that they will feel free to offer comments and share information. This can be accomplished by using "icebreaker" activities or by using other learning technologies to prepare the group members for the content of the case study and the concepts involved as well as to give them some experience in working together. The prospect of using a case study may cause some concern among the participants; they may have questions about why they are there, why a case study is being used, or the process itself. It is best if these concerns and questions are dealt with directly, before the case study is presented.

Presenting a Case Study

Orientation

The first item on the agenda is to introduce the goals of the session and to describe how the case study will be used. It is very important to stress the benefits of the case-study method but also to establish clear expectations at the beginning of the session. The participants need to understand that a case study is not a "game"; it is work—the work of the manager or professional in the case and the organization being studied. The participants should be encouraged to accept responsibility for working through the case. The process is not intended to be easy; in fact, if it is fun it probably is too simple for the group or is not being done correctly.

The facilitator can describe briefly how a case is researched and prepared. A case is a statement of relevant facts about a particular situation but, just as in real life, some facts about the situation are not known. This may be because the cost or effort involved in obtaining such information is too great for the organization or the individual. It may be that the situation is current and the outcome still is unknown. In most cases, information that does not impinge directly on the case has been omitted deliberately. It is the participants' job to define key issues, interrelationships, and problems; to consider alternative solutions and their possible consequences; and to decide on courses of action. This task is complicated. The participants must examine the interrelationships between facts. They must gather data and decide which data is most relevant and valid before attempting to engage in problem solving, decision making, or action planning.

The facilitator also needs to point out that few, if any, cases have one diagnosis, in terms of either the problem issues or the recommended solutions. A strong point of the case-study method is that it requires the group to consider several points of view within the case (e.g., the people actually involved in the case situation, people in other departments, the overall organization, customers, shareholders, etc.) as well as the input of all participants in the training group before proceeding. This is a good time to stress that the purpose of the activity is not to determine what is right, but to acknowledge and work with the existence of *multiple realities*. Because they exist in any business or human interaction or situation, there may be multiple solutions. The purpose of the participants in a case study, then, is not to "decide on" but to "find."

Facilitating

The written case then is distributed. The participants may have been given the case study to read (some time) before the session, or time can be allowed for them to read it as soon as it is distributed. Each participant should read the case individually; the facilitator can summarize what the participants have read; then time can be allotted for all to ask questions. This is one point at which it is critical that the facilitator be thoroughly familiar with the case. However, the facilitator should stick to answering questions about the process or the written case at this point. It is not the time to elaborate details or facts or to begin to solve the problem for the participants. There may be some differences in the way participants interpret the written case, and this is a valid subject for further discussion and learning. The facilitator should not defend the case. If participants question the personality, attitudes, and ways of doing things of the manager or professional who is the subject of the case study, the facilitator can point out that, just as in real life, individual personalities are organizational variables (Towl, 1969; Willings, 1968).

How the facilitator chooses to start the case discussion may depend on the participants' existing knowledge and experience or their levels of readiness. One method of approaching the case analysis, suggested by Willings (1968) is to first conduct small-group discussions of the case. To increase involvement, start by asking the participants to discuss what is happening in the case organization or situation. Also ask them to identify what is negative and what is positive about the situation. Allow a specific amount of time for these small-group discussions.

The next step is a total-group discussion led by the facilitator. This would begin with a discussion of the small-group work, starting with what the participants think is relevant in the case. The facilitator would list points on newsprint and ask *why* participants think that particular facts are relevant. One of the skills to be developed might be stated as pinpointing the *real* problem or issues. The participants may need to be reminded to think about the purpose, goal, or objective of the person and/or organization in the case study. They should be encouraged to think of the case situation as though they were actually part of it—rather than looking on from the outside—and to try to feel the constraints and pressures that are on individuals in real situations.

During this and subsequent discussions, the facilitator's task is to monitor the direction of the discussion but not its content. In the case method, the facilitator is not an instructor in the conventional sense and does not insert "expert" advice or facts into the case discussion. It is important to allow the participants to express a variety of viewpoints and ideas. There will be varying degrees of participation, and some participants will contribute more than others. The participants will evaluate the case within their own frames of reference and relate it to their own knowledge and experiences. To encourage them to do this, the facilitator must establish norms of openness, inquiry, and experimentation. He or she needs to make sure that the participants understand that there are no right or wrong answers, that the learning comes from providing each participant an opportunity to discuss with other how they think and feel about the problem and to compare his or her thoughts with those of others. Therefore, it is imperative that all points of view are covered, so the discussion is not shortchanged.

The facilitator also should not attempt to speed up the process. Participants need time to think about ideas and new concepts, make associations, and so on (especially if this is the first time they have engaged in a case study). Without this synthesis, and if they feel "pushed," they may jump to conclusions rather than analyze and evaluate.

The participants may need to be advised of several analytical "truths" at this point. The first is that *the stated or "presenting" problem is not always (maybe even rarely is) the actual problem*. The second is that *symptoms are not causes*. The third is that *the stated problem may be technical, whereas the real problem may be human*. Participants often focus on concrete facts (dates, schedules, memos, etc.) and fail to take personalities into consideration. They may need to be advised to think about the situation in terms of people as well as facts, to take another look at what individuals in the situation are doing. One typical problem that often is overlooked is how people interact. They can be asked to consider who is really running things, what the pressures (from above and below) are on various individuals, what things people have in common, and what the motivating and demotivating factors are (Willings, 1968). Of course, it is possible that the participants will become "stuck" on human relations problems when other issues are more important. The facilitator also needs to help the participants to distinguish between their own personal values and theories and the facts of the case, to separate the data from their ideas about the data. The facilitator may ask the participants to discuss the pros and cons of the actions taken in the case or, when asking the participants to identify what they think is the real problem, the facilitator can ask for evidence to support each conclusion.

Cognitive Input

During the group discussion, the facilitator may provide cognitive input in the form of lecturettes, handouts, visual aids, and so on to describe various theories and show various models (e.g., decision-making and problem-solving models) in relation to the case study. For example, the facilitator may deliver a lecturette, with visual aids, on force-field analysis or may focus on a specific skill area that pertains to the case. This cognitive input is intended to guide the participants' thinking and to develop their skills in analyzing situations, asking pertinent and useful questions, and identifying and scrutinizing possible solutions. The facilitator may tell the participants that the purpose of presenting the concepts, theories, and/or models is to enable the participants to *use* them, not just to understand them. This ability to utilize and apply knowledge suitably is one of the primary aims of the case-study method. Therefore, it is the participants' job to decide which concept or theory fits the specific situation and how it best can be applied.

In some circumstances, the facilitator also may be able to show videotapes or films of actual interviews with people in the case study or of parts of the case organization at work (e.g., meetings or processes). These audiovisual components should be pertinent to the case material and edited so that they are not repetitious or boring. The opportunity to read about some important aspect of the case and then see it in action can serve to enhance the participants' feeling for the case organization and the reality of the case.

It is important that all participants understand what is going on in the case before the facilitator shifts the discussion to what should be done about it. As the group members talk, the facilitator should list points, people, characteristics, and so on, on newsprint flip charts. He or she also can make charts and diagrams to show procedures and relationships between people and facts, patterns of interaction, and the like. These newsprint posters help to focus the discussion and also serve a reminders of what has been discussed and of the content that they represent.

The participants should not be allowed to discuss solutions prematurely, but neither should they be allowed to "massage" the data excessively. If the participants get sidetracked in theoretical discussions, the facilitator can redirect them to what is going on, e.g., ask them to examine significant relationships or external stress-inducing factors. One of the facilitator's tasks is to assess where the group is and to control the momentum of the discussion. A discussion group easily can become carried away in overanalyzing or, at the other extreme, in jumping to impulsive action before the analysis has been completed. It is necessary to maintain a balance between the two. Once the group has identified the primary problem(s), it probably is appropriate to focus on possible secondary and tertiary problems.

Action Planning

At some point, the facilitator may have to shift from listing issues or facts to discussing primary points and evaluating them. A clue that this is necessary is when the discussion becomes repetitious. The facilitator then should shift the focus from general to more specific, to move the group on to action planning. The facilitator can say, "Yes, but what do you *do* about this now?" The participants are encouraged to discuss possible ways of handling the problem while the facilitator lists them all on newsprint. The facilitator can ask questions such as, "What would happen if (a particular person in the case) were to do (a specific action)?" The facilitator may need to introduce new concepts, challenge old concepts, or question a particular line of thought as the group works. He or she can ask what the person in the case has done, what the person *should* have done, and what he or she can do now. The group members can be allowed a few minutes to think about what they would do to solve the problem(s). They then suggest ways to solve each problem previously identified as being important (ways to improve the situation). Some participants may even cite their own organization's policy in dealing with this type of situation. The various points of view should provide new insights to the group. It is unlikely that all members of the group will agree on a course of action, but each participant should be expected to make his or her own decision.

In the ensuing analysis, the possible consequences of each action are listed and those that are unacceptable for some reason are eliminated. This consideration of cause and effect is very important. For each suggested action, the possible effects should be identified. The facilitator can help by asking questions such as "If you do (a specific action), will something else also need to be done (e.g., boost sales, expand a plant or distribution system)?" "What restrictions are there in terms of capacity, money, people, and other resources?" "What time restraints are present?" The participants may need to be reminded that people can *talk about* making things happen much faster than they can *actually be made* to happen. The group also should consider the costs (personal, financial, time, and other) of solutions considered as well as other impacts (e.g., would there be a legal basis to fire somebody?) (Towl, 1969). Finally, the group arrives at a final statement of diagnosis and solution, complete with likely results, effects, and implications.

Follow-up

Once the participants have identified the solution(s) to the problem, the facilitator can tell them how the problem was handled in the actual organization and what the outcome was, disguising any identities that might violate the confidentiality of the case study. It is possible that some participants may become defensive at this point because they have invested time and energy into developing a solution to which they have become committed. It may be necessary to reiterate the fact that there is rarely one "right" way to solve any problem, and that a training group's solution may be no better or no worse than the one that actually was tried.

In processing the experience, the facilitator can ask a series of questions to highlight the major conceptual points and to reinforce new learnings and new skills. These questions should draw out points related to the objectives or goals of the training session. The facilitator can summarize the points of the discussion and ask the participants to make generalizations and state principles about dealing with similar organizational problems. Then the participants can be asked to describe similar problems in their own jobs and to state how they would handle them in light of what they have learned from the case-study activity.

Case Studies in Program Development

A case study needs to be supplemented with the use of lectures or lecturettes, flip charts, readings, handouts, films or videos, and other types of experiential learning such as structured experiences, role plays, simulations, practice sessions, and actual experience. The design of the training program should include a change of pace, a sequence that balances types of input and output. In planning this, it is important to keep in mind the amount of time available for the entire training program and the amount of time required to complete the case study.

The Harvard program mentioned in the "history" portion of Chapter 1 asked professors to plan their courses with a carefully sequenced series of "decision points." Thus, the purpose is not only to teach specific knowledge but to teach the ability to *use* knowledge and information, to make critical analyses and decisions. Specific information may become obsolete; the ability to assimilate, analyze, and use information does not (Towl, 1969).

Towl also states that after much experimentation and work over many years, the interaction between cases and concepts was summarized as follows by the professors involved in the Harvard program:

1. Building a ready reserve or "repertoire" of cases;
2. Converting a topic outline to a matrix for case analysis;
3. The case-concept-case sandwich;
4. Currently useful distinctions (e.g., between job satisfaction and productivity);
5. Course concepts as the magnetic field for case discussion;
6. Formulating concepts from case discussion.

It is important to note that this work also pointed up the fact that participants were not ready to see meaningful conceptual relationships until they had experienced enough *shared* case discussion.

Sources of Cases

The Inter-Collegiate Case Clearing House (ICH), Soldier's Field, Boston, Massachusetts, publishes, lists, and distributes cases. For example, their *Inter-Collegiate Bibliography, Selected Cases, Business Administration*, lists books of cases from commercial publishers in the field of business administration. There are a multitude of published cases in many areas, including corporate strategy, strategic management, organizational behavior, decision making, administration (business, hospital, public, etc.), personnel, human resource management, communication, business ethics, nursing, occupational therapy, vocational education, psychology, and so on. Many case books are available from commercial publishers. These usually can be found in libraries and in other listings under "Cases in. . ." and may be cross-referenced by field (e.g., "Cases in Strategic Management" or "Strategic Management, Cases in. . ."). Further resources are listed in the "References and Bibliography" section of this book.

3

Developing Case Studies

To Write or To Buy

It is accepted practice in many colleges and universities for professors to develop case material. In these settings, research assistants (usually doctoral candidates) often write or help to write cases. The rationale for this is that it helps to train them in case work before they become professors and that it relieves the schedules of busy professors. However, close supervision is needed, and many professors prefer to do their own cases or to have their research assistants accumulate the data and do the drafts, at which point the professors take over. This allows the development of more cases, and the new knowledge in the field can be valuable. However, the lack of business experience on the part of the case writers is unfortunate.

Cases that are intended to be used for training purposes do not need to contain all the details that are required in research reports. In research, too, multiple cases often are required to prove the point. In training, only one case is used, the requirement being that it contain enough pertinent material to stimulate discussion among the participants and enable them to analyze the data and reach valid conclusions.

In the field of HRD, there is controversy over combining research and case writing with consulting. Many consultants have obtained permission to use cases they have worked on. However, because this combination can "backfire" in a number of ways, the consultant who plans to combine consulting with case research must be very careful to establish *clear expectations* with the client contact and the organization.

One of the reasons that case research is a touchy subject is that it costs the organization that is being studied in several ways. There can be negative fallout later from the content of the case, even if every attempt has been made to make it subjective. Personnel are distracted from their usual work to provide information to the case researcher. There are costs to the case researcher, too. These include the costs of being on site (mostly in terms of time, but also in salaries, miscellaneous expenses, travel, writing and revising, transcription and secretarial time, review, getting releases, reproducing and print-ing the case, and so on). In fact, the difficulty of conducting case research in a real organization and the expertise required to write cases precludes most users from doing it. In many circumstances, it is better to buy cases.

If, however, the decision is made to research and develop a case study, it is best to start by selecting a simple case situation, not one that includes complex or obscure issues. The beginning case writer can read good cases and analyze them for technique, content, and presentation. When the actual draft is ready, it should be shown to more experienced users, peers, and colleagues. Their comments, insights, and suggestions for revision then can be incorporated in-to further drafts. Finally, the writer can actually use the case with a group and learn from what happens.

The following section describes the stages in developing a case study.

Research

The task of finding a suitable organization on which to base the case study; collecting the appropriate and necessary data from in-dividuals, groups, and other sources in the organization; checking the facts; and obtaining a release may well take more time and ef-fort than the actual writing of the case study.

It is easier to coordinate the process if the person who does the research is the one who will actually write the case but, for several reasons, this is not always possible. If the case study is being written as a team effort, the planning and coordination become even more critical.

Planning

Good planning is an essential part of the case-development effort. First, the researcher must consider the need for the case. What are the topics, concepts, theories, and models to be taught? What are the types of issues to be considered? What type of problem is to be illustrated? What field or area of organizational endeavor is most appropriate? What other special considerations are there?

Search for Organization and Issue

Once the need for the case has been identified, the next step is to search for an appropriate organization and issue around which a case can be written to fill that need. It is difficult to find organizations in which executives are willing to talk about problems and solutions. Finding appropriate leads is a research task in itself. One possible source of leads is people who have been involved in cases that you have written in the past. People who are also in the business (consultants, etc.) get leads through their work and contacts; they often will be glad to tell you about any possibilities. You can solicit leads from peers, colleagues, people in professional networks, other business contacts, former students, and people you meet at conferences and seminars. You also can read articles in professional journals and business newspapers, which frequently run articles about organizations that have or have solved interesting problems.

When soliciting leads, it is important to specify that you need to know *who to contact in the organization* and what the issue is. Even if a lead results in a good contact, the person's organization may not be appropriate for a case study or agreeable to your conducting one. However, the contact person may be able to help you to find another contact person in another organization.

Initial Contact

Before calling or writing to the contact person, check your information. Is the situation in the organization suitable for your case study? Has a case on it already been done? Do some research on the company so that you are not going in "cold." If you write a letter, emphasize that the case will be used for education and that it will make a contribution to the field (e.g., management, medicine, nursing, engineering). Thank the contact person in advance for any cooperation and help. You may want to send a sample case with your letter, stating that all cases are different and briefly outlining what you hope to achieve with your case (Leenders & Erskine, 1973).

Then make an appointment with the contact person. Have a specific proposal when you go in. Let the contact person know what you are looking for. Provide information about what the case study will be and do, what type of training program or course you expect to use it in, the goals of the session (what you want to teach the participants or students), and how you use cases. Emphasize the unique value of what the particular organization and situation can bring to the case that is worthy of study as well as the contribution that it will make to education. In some instances, a case study can provide good publicity for the organization, stressing how it has handled the problem.

It is a good idea to get an overview of the problem situation early on in order to check the feasibility of going ahead with the case-study research. Later, it is important to get a chronological overview.

Each time you meet with the contact person, describe how you see the case evolving and continue to do this throughout the process, to clarify what is happening and what might happen so that the contact person's and organization's expectations will not be different from yours. Outline your method of operation, the timing, and your needs from the organization. Stress that a case writer must remain neutral and will not participate in the actual solving or analysis of the problem, i.e., you will not be present to serve as a consultant. In some situations, the case writer may be the person who actually will be using the case and may be in a position to provide feedback later to the subject organization on how the participants viewed or solved the problem, but this is rare.

Discuss how much disguise will be involved in writing the case. It may or may not be necessary to disguise the organization, the product or service, the location, the people involved, certain actions, and company data such as turnover, production, or sales figures. The section that follows on "Writing" will help to clarify some of the issues around the subject of disguise.

Another expectation to be established is whether the other executives and managers in the organization are or will be agreeable to the case study—whether they can and will cooperate. You need to make a concerted effort at this point to determine whether you will be able to get the whole picture of the problem issue in the organization. It is best if the contact person is at the top of the organizational hierarchy or can obtain formal approval from the top, so that managers and others in the organization know that you and the case research have been "approved."

Finally, ask who will review the drafts of the case study and sign the release. The release is written permission from the appropriate executive(s) in the organization to use the case (the final, approved draft), to *publish and distribute* it for educational purposes. The case study is useless without written approval and release of content. During the initial contacts, ask the contact person and other top executives, "Will you be willing to have this case published and distributed publically?" You may not want to put in the time and effort required for a good case study if the contact person says that it "will have to be reviewed by our legal department."

Data Collection

A large part of case-study research is a personal interview with each manager, executive, and person who is involved in or has a unique perspective of the case problem or issue. This may include people in various positions or various parts of the organization that may have been affected by the situation, not just those in the section or division in which the problem occurred. Try to find a time that is good for the person being interviewed. Do not focus initially on the "problem"; this can result in embarrassment or defensiveness. Instead, ask about "issues." You can say something like, "I'd like to hear about your experience in dealing with this." Be honest and direct about the information you want, but use tact. This is a good time to practice interviewing skills, including listening skills, observation, and reporting skills. During this process, you often will need to be resourceful in getting the information you need, but you also must be careful not to get a reputation for going over (or under) the head of a particular executive or of looking only for skeletons in closets. Above all, do not give different stories to different people. If your presence is seen is disruptive or subversive, you may be asked to leave. It is better to present yourself as something of a mystery writer who is tracking down clues.

It is best if you can talk to people in the organization while the problem or situation to be studied is occurring or as soon afterward as possible. As in a mystery story, it is more difficult to trace the trail after it is cold. Once an incident is over with (especially if it was an unpleasant one) people minimize or forget their doubts, their problems in dealing with it, their confusions, and so on. While conducting the interview, you may choose to take notes or—if you have an exceptionally good memory—you may make your notes immediately after the interview. Some interviewers prefer to record the interview on audiotape. If you prefer this method, be sure that the person whom you are interviewing is comfortable with it; if not, it may inhibit what that person will discuss or reveal. You will need to assure each person whom you interview that case information will not be discussed with or revealed to anyone outside the organization except for the educational purposes for which the case study is being written. You may want to describe the degree of disguise that will be used and the amount of information (if any) that might be shared with your contact person. If the interviewee agrees to be tape recorded, *get a verbal release on the tape recording* before conducting the rest of the interview.

During the research phase, it is important to remain open enough so that you get all the information that is available and do not attempt to define the problem too soon or cut off avenues of exploration or information. In many cases, the actual problem or situation may be different from what is initially described or from what it initially appears to be. Be prepared for things to arise that you have not previously anticipated. It is important to get *all per-*

tinent data. People tend, either deliberately or unconsciously, to withhold important information. If you think that you are being blocked for some reason, you can rephrase questions so that they appear to be less threatening or less direct. You also can follow up on leads that the person may reveal without realizing it.

One of the problems in doing case research is what to do with confidential information, i.e., information that is pertinent to the case but which the source does not want included in the report. One option is to keep the information in mind, although private, while searching for other leads. Another option is to refuse to accept confidential information. If you say something such as, "I cannot accept confidential information that I cannot use, but all information used in the case study will be disguised (describe how) and used only for educational purposes (describe)," it may overcome the subject's reluctance to release the information.

Another important part of the research task is obtaining a chronological history. This should be done early on and updated throughout the interviewing and research process. The case writer's job is to report the relevant facts of the situation at the time the decision needed to be made or the problem existed. The participants who will use the case-study for educational purposes will be taking the parts of the people involved at the time the situation existed and making decisions as though they were the managers or professionals involved in the issue. Thus, you must be aware of any information that is given as though it were part of the situation but which actually was obtained later or is merely hindsight.

It also is important to obtain file data and other written data as soon as possible, to provide information to be used in interviewing and to check facts and chronological information. Interviews, documents, and personal observation all contribute to an understanding of the facts. People in the organization being studied should not be expected to take the time to provide this data; you may need their help in determining where to find it but you will need to do much of the leg work yourself. In looking for and organizing data, ask yourself, "What will the particiants in the case-study training group need to know?" Of course, you may have to request an expert in the organization to help you to find background or technical data or to explain the data or specific terms or processes to you. Lastly, you may not want to limit your inquiry to data inside the organization. There also may be useful data *outside* the organization. You can ask, "Whom else should I talk to?"

Then, without attempting to draw any conclusions, compare stories. Work until a pattern emerges from the data. Remember that you are looking for *patterns* in the data, not interpretations. Stick to reporting, rather than critiquing, analyzing, judging, or commenting. Above all, *check the facts.*

Finally, remember your responsibility for protecting information obtained for the case study. Do not discuss the organization or the information that you have obtained with other people. In fact, you may be obliged to promise to destroy all case notes and data after you obtain release of the final draft.

A Check List for the Case Researcher

Planning

1. What are the topics, issues, problems, concepts, theories, and/or models to be taught/considered?

Search

1. What contacts can you ask for leads? To what articles or publications can you write to follow up on leads?
2. Have you asked for the name of a *contact* person?

Initial Contact

1. Does your information indicate that the organization is suitable for your study?
2. Have you sent a letter, with a sample case, to the contact person? Have you asked for an appointment?
3. For your first meeting, have you prepared a proposal for the research project, described the value of the case, etc.?
4. Have you obtained an overview of the problem situation from the contact person?
5. Have you exchanged and clarified expectations with the contact person?
6. Have you explained your method of operation and your needs to the contact person? Does he or she seem to understand?
7. Has the contact person told you who will approve the written case and who will sign the release?

Data Collection

1. Have you conducted a personal interview with each person involved in or affected by the issue?
2. Have you asked about "issues" rather than "problems"?
3. Have you established clear expectations about confidentiality and disguise?
4. Have you avoided being manipulative?
5. Have you followed up promptly on leads?
6. Have you remained open and not attempted to define the problem prematurely?
7. Have you included all *pertinent* details?
8. Have you indicated a chronological order of events?
9. Have you checked file data and other written data?
10. Have you reported, but not evaluated, the pattern that has emerged from the data?

Writing

The next steps are organizing the data and writing the first draft of the case study. First, it is necessary to sort the information that you have obtained. Next, you need to organize those materials and notes. Plan the presentation. Prepare an outline of the case. Then you can begin to put the information back together in logical order.

In creating a case study, you will need both writing skills and editing skills. You will need to use good grammar, correct punctuation, etc. It is preferable to use the active voice. Some case writers think that you should use present tense as much as possible in order to foster participant involvement; others say that use of the past tense suggests that the situation may have changed in the case organization and keeps the case from being dated. Obviously, one must use one's own judgment about this, based on the nature of the particular case.

Begin the case study with an introduction that tells what the potential users (the participants in a training group) need to know: what the case is about what they are supposed to do with it. Clearly identify the issues in the case and state why case is presented and how it can be used. You may wish to state that the report is based on a real organization that has cooperated fully in the development of the case, although the organization will remain anonymous and certain facts, names, and so on, have been disguised. In order to protect yourself legally, you may choose to include the standard disclaimer ("any resemblance to actual. . . .").

The written case can be short or long, simple or complex, with a narrow or broad focus, and can deal with a specific skill area or with general administrative skills in a particular field, based on its intended use and the level of knowledge and experience of the potential users. Leenders & Erskine (1973) suggest that the optimum size for a case is a maximum of ten to fifteen pages. A case that is longer may contain more information than the potential users can absorb and apply.

Any outstanding facts about the case should be presented in an overview at the beginning. This includes the most important information about the setting and the people involved. You may mention that only facts that are pertinent to the case and that relate to the issue have been reported and that these will include the historical background of the company; its current situation (profitability, growth, market share, etc., as appropriate); the problem or issue to be dealt with; the current situation; its effect on people; the nature of their jobs or their positions in relation to the problem; and what people have done about the problem so far or how they are reacting to it.

A case study is an attempt to recreate the reality of an organization using only the important and pertinent information and descriptions. The written case must present a wide range of facts, emotions, interactions, physical realities, and other data (including, perhaps, technical data). It also must appeal to the people who will be using it. It must provide the users with clues that enable them to analyze the situation and to make informed recommendations.

One way to begin is to use the present problem and show how it developed, filling in the background needed to understand the organization, the people, and so on. This may include the formal organizational structure or hierarchy, the actual (informal) hierarchy or relationships, physical layouts, and sequences of operations. As in a mystery book, there should be a time structure and a sequence of events. In fact, the case study probably will be easiest to read and understand if it is written somewhat like a story, although more concise and with more narrative and less dialog.

It is not necessary—in fact, it is counterproductive—to include unnecessary descriptions or details. Allow the readers to identify a basic theme and perhaps one or two secondary themes. Do not embellish; a case study is based on facts, and the reader almost always can sense when something does not "ring true" (Willings, 1968). There is a fine line between involving the readers in the case and overloading or boring them. Biographical data about the people in the case generally is not very important; what matters is what they have *done,* what they are doing, and how they think or what they have said about the issues or problem and the other people in the case. Use the topical areas in your outline of the case and flesh them in, but do not overdo it. It also is a good idea to work consistently so you can keep your ideas and themes connected.

The Element of Disguise

It almost always is necessary to preserve the anonymity of the case organization and the people in it; therefore, it almost always is necessary to disguise their identities, keeping only the events and facts that relate to the issues. There are many reasons for this. Some of them are suggested by Leenders & Erskine (1973):

1. To prevent embarrassment and possible loss of business, market status, or credibility of the case organization;
2. To prevent embarrassment and possible adverse impact on the careers of the individuals involved;
3. To keep the organization's competitors from obtaining confidential information and data;
4. To keep case-study participants and others from contacting the organization to "find out what really happened"—a source of harrassment.

The case organization is most likely to request some form of disguise if the issues or actions in the case are controversial, if the report could affect the people involved, or if the publication of the case could affect subsequent events. The most obvious form of disguise is to change the name of the organization. It frequently (but not always) may be necessary to change the names of the people in the case. Depending on the nature of the case problem and the organization, it may or may not be advisable to change the nature of the product or industry. Many people believe that one cannot disguise the nature of the organization without losing or obscuring one of the most salient features of the case. However, some organizations in the United States are so well known that they would be recognized immediately by the case users if the nature of their business or service were not disguised. In such a circumstance it may be necessary to change the description of the product or service to another in the same basic area of endeavor (e.g., an alcoholic-treatment center to a weight-loss center; a manufacturer of one type of appliance to that of another type of appliance). Different cases have different areas of sensitivity. Discussion with the contact person and top executives of the case organization about the amount and nature of disguise needed can help to clear up these issues and establish clear expectations before the case-writing process actually begins. A case is of no use if it is not released.

More subtle forms of disguise include changing dates and locations, if this can be done without destroying important facts. Changing the region of the country in which the organization is located is difficult because it affects the labor situation, wage rates, climate, transportation, market, local regulations, and so on. Inventory and sales figures, turnover statistics, and other data that would benefit competitors of the organization frequently must be disguised. Sometimes this can be accomplished by multiplying *all* figures by a constant such as .93 or 1.1 (Leenders & Erskine, 1973). In some cases, only certain types of disguise are required; i.e., it may be possible to reveal the identity of the organization and merely change the names of the people or to change identities but keep facts and financial data. What usually does not work is to change the job descriptions or positions of key figures in the case or to disguise one department so that people are likely to think that it is another one in the same organization. It probably is easiest to disguise all salient facts or none at all. As would be expected, more complicated cases are harder to disguise.

Just the Facts, Please

In writing the case, stick to factual details, even if you alter or manipulate those details. Use your creativity to disguise, not to invent. Check for consistency in disguising people, organizations, etc. Use what actually happened to focus on the themes that you have identified.

It is not a good idea to attempt to write about a particular field (e.g., chemicals, law, engineering, publishing, banking, etc.) without getting the technical details as well as the facts straight. These details may include laws, regulations, competition, pricing, the market, and so on. Disguised details especially can slip you up. The participants who are using the case study will spot inaccuracies and focus on them, which will distract them from the purpose of using the case study at the least. It also will cause problems of credibility for the facilitator who is using the case study. Even inaccuracies in little details can do this; another reason not to use details that are not pertinent or necessary. To avoid this, have an expert check the draft of the written case. Then revise it.

It is not the job of case writer to point out his or her own point of view, opinions, preferences, evaluations, or solutions. Of course, all researchers will have some prior experience, knowledge, interests, and theories that will influence their perceptions, even if they are scrupulous about trying not to let them interfere with how the case is reported. Similarly, all case writers will form opinions about the cases on which they work. However, it is imperative to the learning objectives of the case-study method that the writer does not allow his or her perceptions or pet theories to be evident in the written case. The purpose of the written case is to supply the information that will enable the case participants to take on the problems and circumstances of the people in the case.

Neither should facts be hidden or obscured. It is very important to keep the objectives of the case study in mind. Even if the case is complicated or there is more than one issue, the participants should be able to find clues and determine what is relevant. If there are too many unnecessary facts or the issues are not clear, the participants easily can become sidetracked and lose much of the benefit of the training. The purpose of the case-study method is not to build "detecting" skills but to develop the participants' skills in selecting which information is important and in analyzing and evaluating that information.

In presenting the case history, the writer should include nonverbal data. This may include nonverval communications and avenues and patterns of communication within the organization. It also includes the values, norms, and attitudes—the operating assumptions —that exist within the organization and its relevant subsections. It includes things that are not said (but may be implied) and the context in which something is said, not just whether or not it is true. The participants who use the case study may use this information to determine *why* they think something was said. It also is important to report the opinions of people in the case as opinions, not as facts. All quotations should be reported as direct quotations, not paraphrased or interpreted, and the person who spoke should be identified. The case writer also should note patterns but not interpret them. Such patterns include what people have done and are doing and the people with whom they do it. If possible, include the conditions under which people act and what the outcomes of their actions might mean to them and others. All factors that can affect the situation should be included, whether these factors be physical or human ones. The timing and sequence of events must be keep clear, and *all sources of data must be identified.*

Additional facts to include are data relating to the organization and flow of work; the sequence of operations; task-relevant interactions; pressures on groups, departments, and executives; financial data; the amount of inventory and raw materials; sales data; marketing plans; and relevant physical factors such as the amount and age of equipment and physical layouts. Diagrams, charts, tables, and figures can be used to illustrate or clarify important points and to add interest. These and other illustrative materials such as reprinted data should appear in the text at the point at which they are pertinent to the case.

In describing the people in the case, be careful not to use stereotypes. The people who use the case will resent or suspect them. It is all right to describe typical behaviors of people and their roles, but not in terms of ethnic or sexual or job stereotypes. In fact, avoid doing anything that could detract from the realism of the case and cause the users not to take it seriously. For example, if you are disguising the identity of the organization or the people in it, do not substitute humorous names. This may be acceptable in some structured experiences and other interventions, but not in case studies.

One of the most difficult challenges of writing a case study is supplying all the information that is needed without overdoing it, without giving the participants more than they can absorb and use. A written case should be significant, interesting, and complete but not overwhelming. The participants need enough to arouse their interest and generate discussion, but there must be room for them to ask questions and generate alternatives. The case writer cannot expect to give the participants all the information that a person in the actual case organization would have, nor is it necessary to do so. Too much information is as bad as too little.

The case writer should stop the case description at the point where action is to be taken. The participants in the case will take over from that point. They should not be directed toward a particular solution or course of action.

Notes for the Facilitator

Many case studies, especially those that are published in a book of cases, contain a section of "Notes for the Facilitator" (generally called "teaching notes" in a case study prepared for a college course). This usually includes suggestions for using the case study: the degree of experience or prior knowledge needed by participants to use the case effectively; how and where the case might be used in a training sequence; and what other facilitators have tried and what happened (e.g., things that worked or did not work). The writer may use this opportunity to suggest different ways of using the case study, different focusus, questions, different alternatives or solutions, and so on. This section often contains a summary of the actual actions that were taken in the case organization and the results. However, other information about the case that the participants do *not* have should not be provided. If the facilitator should use such information, the participants most likely would call "foul." The case writer also should resist this last opportunity to analyze the case or to prescribe a solution. In fact, no information should be included that would serve to *limit* the creativity or possibilities of the users.

As each facilitator uses the case, he or she can add to this section, noting insights, ideas generated by the participants, and answers that he or she may want to remember in the future. If a case is to be used more than once by the members of a training staff, all can benefit from the comments added each time a case is used about how to handle it. Each facilitator must remember that each group is different; notes from past training sessions do not provide assurance of how any new session will turn out. At the least, this section can help facilitators in selecting cases to use.

Revising

When the initial writing of the case study is completed, it is a good idea to set it aside for a brief period of time—to distance oneself from it—in order to gain objectivity before reviewing the draft and preparing to revise it. However, this should not be so long that the details are no longer fresh. No matter how satisfied one is with the first draft, one can be sure that it requires a lot of revision.

There are many objectives of the revision process. The first task is to scrutinize the way in which information is presented and to eliminate unnecessary information. The case must be looked at through the eyes of the users. Does the draft include all the information that is needed to analyze the case? Is the information clear? Is it aided by visual representations when appropriate? Have you "taken sides" among the personalities involved, analyzed the information rather then merely presenting it, slanted anything, etc.? Conversely, is there *too much* information? Are charts, tables, and other data presented unnecessarily?

Next, check to see that the information is presented in an order that makes sense. This may not be chronological order, but the chronology should be apparent. It should be remembered that the case study is a training tool. One must always keep the possible training objectives in mind. A good case makes the facilitator's job easier.

A Check List for the Case Writer

Writing

1. Have you sorted and organized your materials and notes? Have you prepared an outline of the case?
2. Does your introduction tell the case users what the case is about and what they are to do with it?
3. Have you started with an overview of the salient facts of the case and what will be included?
4. Does the case begin at a logical point (e.g., with a statement of the presenting problem)?
5. Have you included all necessary information: the organizational structure, people, roles, relationships, operating assumptions, financial data, sales and marketing data, physical layouts, nature and sequence of operations, pressures, time and sequence of events, etc.? Did you stick to the facts, without embellishing or interpreting?
6. Have you included charts, diagrams, figures, etc., where appropriate?
7. Have you deleted unnecessary descriptions, dialog, and details?
8. Have you disguised the organization consistently and in accordance with your discussions with the contact person?
9. Has your technical data been checked by experts in the field?
10 Are you including notes for the facilitator?

Revising

1. Does the case contain all the information that is needed by the users? Is it presented in logical order?
2. Have you eliminated unnecessary information?
3. Have your checked your word usage, spelling, punctuation, grammar, sentence and paragraph structure, etc.?
4. Has the draft been reviewed by an experienced case writer or an expert in the field of the case organization?
5. Has the draft been reviewed by your contact person?

The next objective is to *edit*. This involves rereading and further revision. This is the time to check the spellings and meanings of words and to clarify sentences. To paraphrase an old line, what you said may not be what you meant. Also check sentence and paragraph structure. Few sentences or paragraphs cannot be made more succinct or polished. Take a look at the writing style. If necessary, consult *The Elements of Style* (Strunk & White, 1979), *The Chicago Manual of Style* (University of Chicago Press), the *United States Government Printing Office Style Manual*, or a similar reference. Once you have revised the content, reread the text one last time to check the spelling, grammar, and punctuation (you will be less likely to get "hung up" on content if you focus on these separately).

When you have compeleted your revision of the first draft, ask a colleague or an expert in the field to review it. Make any necessary revisions before submitting it to your contact person in the case organization. Ask *this* person to evaluate the case in light of *anything that might interfere with obtaining a release* by the organization.

Getting the Release

You must obtain a formal, written release, signed by an authorized representative of the case organization, before the case can be published and distributed. Your contact person should be able to identify potential problems before the written case is turned over to other executives (up the hierarchy) for review. Several people in the organization (executives other than your contact person) may want to review the final draft of the case before agreeing to release it for publication. If you have the opportunity, let each person know that the case has been reviewed by others and who they are. Any of these people may suggest rewording, additions, and/or deletions. They are apt to strutinize financial data, information about new products or plans, and direct quotations. It may be necessary for you to reassure these people that all information about the organization except the written text of the case will be held strictly confidential. (In fact, you may be required to destroy your notes and backup materials.)

Most releases are for publication and distribution for educational purposes only. The case writer or the organization for which he or she works usually obtains copyright to the case. The text of the written release should include a statement that the case (with the title named) has been read by authorized representatives of (name of case organization). It should also state that "I (we) authorize use by" (name of case writer or organization that will claim copyright) "to print, copyright, distribute, and use the written case in educational or training programs" (or for educational or training purposes) "without change." The official signature(s) should be followed by the person's name, title, organization, etc., and the date of signing. Of course, these guidelines are general; the specific wording may vary with each case.

4

A Background for Using Simulations in Human Resource Development

What a Simulation Is and What It Is Not

Although the classic definition of simulation is a representation of something, in most applications today, simulation tends to mean the testing or use of a model. Models themselves represent, they do not explain. By represent, we mean that a model depicts or mirrors some aspect of reality (the form, not necessarily the content) and shows the interrelationships or processes of the component parts of the model, sometimes over time. In fact, a simulation is both a model and a process. Process implies change, and in the use of almost all simulations in business or education, some factors of the model are changed in order to study the effects. For our purposes, then, a simulation is a process based on a model of a process, an *operating* model of a real system or a model of change in the system. It is one form of modeling. (For more on models, see *Using Lecturettes, Theory, and Models in Human Resource Development,* the third book in this University Associates Training Technologies collection.)

There are several types of simulations. These include the following:

1. *Verbal model.* This is a *description* (oral or, more often, written) of relationships between the components of the model. It may include statistics. It is not as precise as analog, digital, or mathematical models. Furthermore, because the person who writes the model selects the words to be used,

it may be slanted, consciously or unconsciously, toward that person's point of view.

2. *Diagrammic models.* These consist of representations such as pictures, maps, and diagrams (including flow diagrams). They are more flexible than mathematical models and more specific than verbal descriptions. They allow alternatives to be depicted by a "branching mode" (see the description of a decision tree in Chapter 5). Such models are used in urban renewal, traffic engineering, other types of engineering, organizations, computer programming, and military war games. Computer graphics have greatly enhanced the possibilities and creatability of diagrammic models.

   One specific type of diagrammic model that is being used more and more is the flow chart or flow diagram, a depiction of the sequential and dynamic aspects of a situation or problem, i.e., its behavior over time. Such diagrams permit recycling but not simultaneous processes. A flow diagram can be an entity in itself or part of a more complex simulation.

3. *Analog models.* These include representations or simulations of physical realities. Although the term "analog" most often is applied to all such models, in fact, a model that has the same properties as the original but a change in scale is an "iconic" model. An example of this is a smaller-scale physical model—such as an architectural model—that represents the physical *appearance* of something (i.e., shape and dimensions). A true analog model (from the word "analogy") implies representation by other properties. Many analog models, such as wind tunnels, replicate physical *conditions or effects* (such as, for example, wind velocity or pressure).

4. *Analytical or mathematical model.* In this type of model, the referent system or reality is represented by a set of equations with measurable variables. This typically is used when numbers are a major part of the reality and the user wants to determine probability. Such uses include accounting, financial and economic forecasting, strategic planning, distribution, supply and demand, and other business applications. Mathematical models have been used for a long

time in written form by organizations and universities for business training and by the military for purposes of allocation and tactical warfare. Although they are used in some psychological studies, they are not suited to the study of human relations problems because of the difficulty in quantifying behavior. In training, their primary use is in the calculations necessary for two-person, zero-sum games.

5. *Digital simulations.* More simulations than models, these are totally computerized. They are much more complicated than written mathematical models. The computer programmer uses the binary system (zeros and ones) to represent discretely the variables in other realities. However, in creating a digital simulation the programmer must cover every single, pertinent detail, in sequence, because the computer has no imagination. A computer simulation can be *static,* that is, representing a cross-section (a particular point in time), or *dynamic,* representing a time series.

There also are simulations that are hybrids, combinations of analog and digital. The "flight simulators" used to train pilots often are a combination of analog (physical) models and digital simulations.

Verbal models, diagrammic (including charts and pictorial) models, and iconic and analog models are nonsymbolic, as are mathematical or quantitative models such as analytic models (in the mathematical sense, e.g., the economic theory of an organization), and numerical models (e.g., a particular organization's accounting system). Digital simulations, however, are symbolic.

It is important to remember that a model or a simulation of how the model operates is a *representation* of reality; it is *not a duplication of the reality* itself. In particular, behavioral simulations should be regarded as experiments. A simulation is intended to provide experience in working with a system such as the one that is represented, but—as in real life—each experience is different. It is not to be expected that an actual person or a real-life organization will behave exactly as a simulation did.

In most cases, a simulation will include all the factors and variables that are necessary to "run" it, but will not include extraneous data that is present in the referent system but not vital to its operation. For example, in a simulation of a business organization, the titles of the executives who make pertinent decisions may be included, but if the model is primarily economic and not behavioral, there will be no personal information to turn those titles into roles. Many economic business simulations depict a *typical* organization rather than a specific one; because there are no actual role incumbents, background information about the persons who hold various positions will not be included.

A Rationale for Using Simulations

Simulations can be used in human resource develoment for several purposes. They are especially useful in behavioral and economic research to test hypotheses, theories, and models. Because a simulation imitates the real-time behavioral characteristics of a system, it can be used to test hypotheses about what occurs in the system. Predictions can be made, then a simulation can be used to reinforce the existing hypothesis or to develop new hypotheses when cause-and-effect relationships are not clear. A simulation also can be used to validate or compare theories. (For definitions of—and a discussion of the differences between—hypotheses, theories, and models, see *Using Lecturettes, Theory, and Models in Human Resource Development*, the third book in this Training Technologies set.) Theories also can be combined. A simulation can be even more useful in questioning the details of a model. In all these applications, alternatives can be explored, experiments can be made. As questions and possibilities arise, changes can be made, and the simulation can be rerun. Ideas can be expanded. The effect of such use of a simulation is to provide the equivalent of real-time experience in using or manipulating the system, be it an economic model, a model of an organization, or a behavioral model. As will be seen later, this can be particularly useful in teaching and training as well as in research (Guetzkow, Kotler, & Schultz, 1972).

Simulations often are used in business planning and decision making and in resource allocation to predict and study the effect of uncertain variables or additional data. Many of these simulations include stochastic elements or the use of random numbers. (These are discussed in Chapter 5.) In fact, business and administrative science simulations seem to be more "applied" than those in most other areas of social science; such applications combine experimentation and analysis for practical, rather than purely research, purposes. They usually involve the use of computers to measure the effects of variations in input data or structural parameters on output or results. In such uses, the simulation is used to ask "what if?" Different policies and strategies can be used to test the system's response, be it a market, economy, budget, or the like. This can be used to generate best- and worst-case scenarios. Such simulations typically are used in planning to "weigh the odds" and as "trial runs." Related to this are the use of simulations to find the best solutions and the monitoring of a program as it goes along, against simulation projections.

In using a computer for such experiments, in addition to having an accurate simulation, one must program in the probable effects of proposed actions. As has been stated previously, the computer has no imagination; it will not supply assumptions or details.

Another use of simulations that resembles the business applications is that of training. Social or organizational systems are simulated either by physical means or computer program, and the participants enact typical roles that would be found in such a system. In management training, for example, a physical simulation of an office environment could be created and participants could be assigned the roles of members of the top-management team, given pertinent information about the organization (hospital, museum, bank, agency, manufacturer, etc.), and told to complete some task such as making plans for the next quarter or year. Some simulations are complex "in-basket" activities (see a discussion of this type of activity in *Using Structured Experiences in Human Resource Development,* the first book in this Training Technologies set). If the participant group is large, the players can be divided into teams, each of which represents a department or division within the organization. The simulation then would require each "department" to accomplish some task (such as creating its functional plan for the next year) and also would requre it to exchange information with the other teams in order to accomplish its task. Cooperation and collaboration often are major parts of the learning experience in training simulations.

One useful application of interest to HRD practitioners is the use of simulation to develop consultation skills. According to Boyer (1987), this approach can be used toward the end of the consultant's cognitive education or at the beginning of the practicum phase, to integrate cognitive, interpersonal, and personal skills.

Although the in-basket activity and the design that Boyer describes for training consultants are relatively pure simulations, most training simulations are relatively structured; they have rules and other built-in procedures. These simulations are called "games," and they are discussed in Chapters 6, 7, 8, and 9 of this book. In order to understanding gaming, however, one first must know something about the design and construction of pure simulations.

The History of Simulations

For our purposes, the history of simulations is tied to the history of simulation *games,* which is presented in detail in Chapter 6. The most significant occurrence in the history of simulations is the introduction and growing use of digital computers that began in late 1950s. Before that time, it was difficult to find analogs for business; since then, simulations have become a major tool in business analysis and planning. One of the major uses of simulations in the 1940s and '50s was those that the RAND Corporation and others had developed for use by the military and, later, the diplomatic corps. The first published use of the Monte Carlo method (see definition in Chapter 5) for scientific application appeared in the *Journal of Chemical Physics* in 1953; simulations have been used extensively for scientific inquiry since then.

The first business simulation was created by the American Management Association in 1956; others soon were developed for teaching purposes in major universities (UCLA, Carnegie Tech, Yale, Harvard, Tulane, etc.). In the early 1960s, businesses such as IBM and General Electric also developed simulation games to train their managers and other experts within the frameworks of their particular systems.

In addition, behavioral simulations were developed for use in psychological experiments in the early '60s, beginning with HOMUNCULUS, a computer model of a social person (Gullahorn & Gullahorn, 1972). This simulated how people make behavioral decisions in interactions with others. Other computer models of personality were developed in the late '60s. Personality processes were represented by computer program subroutines. These generate behavioral or verbal outputs in response to inputs. Used first for research in psychiatry, psychology, and psychotherapy, they were expanded to study social organizations, demographics, social policies, information dissemination and diffusion, political (electoral and legislative) processes, international relations, socialization processes, and other group processes as well as individual behavior and decision making.

Most of the early computerized simulations were written in FORTRAN or other general computer languages such as ALGOL, COBOL, and PL/1. Special packages of routines or procedures such as GASP, a FORTRAN subroutine, were developed to be used with these general computer languages for simulations. Later simulations employed various computer simulation languages, developed in the 1970s, such as GPSS, SIMSCRIPT, SIMSCRIPT II, MILITRAN, SIMPAC, and SIMULA. These substantially reduced the amount of time required for programming and debugging, thus reducing the cost of writing simulation programs.

Today, computer simulations are used by businesses, other organizations and economic systems, communities, public services, municipal resources, disaster-relief agencies, public and private transport systems (land, air, and water), traffic engineers, architects, astronauts, social scientists, geologists, diplomats, and the military, and in the fields of education, sociology (particularly demographics), international affairs, medicine, all types of engineering, geography, bioligical science, education, economics, mathematics, nuclear physics, chemistry, ecology, city planning, urban renewal, land use, fish and game management, water resources, forest management, conservation, mining, housing, police communications, and fire prevention, as well as management education and training.

However, the story has not ended. In the past, computers have been limited in that they could compute in a linear fashion only. Now, a new breed of computers based on parallel processing architectures have been developed. These "super computers" can execute more than one instruction simultaneously. This breakthrough opens up heretofore unimaginable possibilities for future computer applications.

5

Developing Simulations

Understanding Aspects of Simulations

Although the majority of actual simulations (as opposed to some board games and other games that are not actually simulations) now used in training are computerized, not all are. It is possible to develop a simulation of a business entity, for example, that can be manipulated by participants with the aid of calculators and without the use of computers. However, more and more training simulations are computerized. Obviously, it would be impossible to actually create a computer simulation without a knowledge of computer programming. However, there is information that nonprogrammers should know if they intend to request or use computerized simulations for training or other purposes. This information also can be helpful in working with programmers to develop new simulations. With the exception of details that are specific to the use of computers, all the information in this section applies to noncomputerized simulations as well. Because this chapter is concerned with simulations as training technologies, we will focus on the development of simulations that will be used for training "games," not those designed for research. However, many characteristics of the two types of simulations are the same.

There are basically two types of simulations used in training: (a) those that deal with economic business concerns and (b) those that deal with behavior. Business and economic simulations primarily are used in training managers. These include not only economic considerations (mathematical) but also interrelationships between the many components of the organization. In training, these components and the variables in them will be manipulated to show the effects of different courses of action. Thus, the basic theories or operating procedures on which the simulation is based must be explicit as well as logical, and the simulation must include all variables and must be able to compute the effects of change in any of those variables. This makes simulations very difficult to construct.

There are three basic focuses in business simulation (Newell & Meier, 1972):

1. *Type of problem.* The focus here is on specific, decision-making aspects of physical and economic systems (e.g., businesses, communities, and service organizations) such as inventory, scheduling, budgeting, and distribution systems.

2. *Scope of System.* These simulations encompass an entire organization rather than parts of the organization. They include its divisions, feedback systems, and individual decision-making processes. The interactions of the various subsystems must be included. However, because it usually would be impossible or impractical to include all the components of an organization, the simulation developers must determine what will be *done* with the information and then decide which operations and what data to include.

3. *Methodology.* This asks what the simulation will be used for, (e.g., practical use such as forecasting or budget setting, or operational gaming for training purposes). For heuristic purposes (e.g., to teach analytic, decision-making, or planning skills), simulations must include the rules of the game, policing and umpiring functions, and other game variables in addition to what is required for pure simulations. These are discussed in Chapters 6, 7, 8, and 9. With each methodology, one must determine what kinds of decisions (changes) will be made, what information will be needed, and what processes are involved.

Stages in Developing a Simulation

Defining the Objectives and the System

The first step is to identify the objectives of the simulation: what it will *do* and how it will be *used*. This may require stating a specific question to be asked, a hypothesis to be tested, effects to be studied, or a problem to be solved. This must be stated explicitly; all terms must be defined, and all criteria must be specified. One must identify the referent system or organization, the business (product or service) that it is in, and provide some background related to the problem or question to be raised.

Constructing the Model

A simulation is a mathematical or physical model of a real system, represented by a set of equations or the physical behavior of an analog. It must accurately represent how the system being modeled actually operates. Simulation results are the responses of the model system to a particular set of initial conditions with *specified interactions between components of the system*. These linkages include inputs and outputs (interactions) between subsystems and to and from the outside environment. Examples of these initial conditions and interactions include organizational (system) policies, management practices, patterns of influence, norms, operations, fixed and variable costs, time periods, and informational and decision-making systems. The model may even contain behavioral information, such as hierarchical power or pressure on people for certain decisions or responses (expressed in percentages).

One of the major problems in developing a simulation is finding sources of valid data and collecting the data that you want to include. Some sources of data are organizational records and reports, interviews with executives and financial personnel, customer or client profiles, market studies, sales figures, economic profiles, competitor analyses, etc. The following is a list of the kinds of data that *may* need to be included in a business simulation.

• absenteeism, accounts payable, accounts receivable, adaptive strategies, administrative expenses, advertising budgets, advertising schedules, age of work force, arrival and departure dates • back orders, balance sheets, bonuses, building permits • capacity per unit, capital equipment, capital investments, carrying costs, cash flow, cash generated, cash required, clerks, collection costs, competition, competitor analyses, computer availability, computer down time, construction costs, consumer demand, costs, credit memos, customer service, customs regulations • damage, delays, departmental budgets, depreciation, distributors, district sales management, dividends, due dates • economic conditions, engineering capability, equipment, expansion, expenses, export regulations • facilities, financial statements, functional analyses, functional plans • geographic considerations, government regulations, gross margin percentage, growth rate • handling costs, health regulations, hierarchy • import regulations, income statements, indirect costs, inspections, insurance, interest rates, inventory levels, investments • job scheduling • labor negotiations, labor rates, labor strikes, lead time, legal considerations, loans • machine load and capacity, machinery, mailing lists, maintenance, manufacturing costs, market growth or decline, market research, market share, marketing budgets, markets available, materials • net profit, new technologies • office supplies, operating costs, orders, overhead • packaging, pay raises, pension or retirement plans, performance in previous quarters, permits, plant capacity, plant investment, postage, pricing, probabilities of occurrence, profit and loss, product image, production capacity, production costs, production rate, production time, production volume • quality control, quotas • raw materials purchased, raw materials recycled, refunds, research and development, retail price, retailers, retooling, returns, royalties • safety regulations, salaries, sales administration, sales commissions, sales distribution, sales estimates, sales forecasts, sales offices, salespersons, scheduling and dispatch, shareholders, shifts, shop performance, set-up time, shipping/dreyage, spoilage, start-up costs, stock, supply and demand, surplus • targeted production, taxes, tax rates, timing, training and development, transportation, travel, turnover • unions, utility costs • vacations, variances, vendors, volume • wait time, warehousing, waste, work force, work load • year-to-date, etc.

The time scale of the simulation may be an important variable. Other variables may include the use of specific planning methods and whether the system to be simulated is in a steady-state, growth, or declining mode.

Endogenous and Exogenous Variables

Some variables are dependent variables that describe the behavior of the system—the results of relationships and interactions—and are built into the model. These are called "endogenous" variables. Examples of these are inventory and production scheduling. Other forces or variables are independent of the state of the system and therefore in the external environment; they are "exogenous." Examples of these are the Dow Jones Average and the value of the dollar. It is important to identify all the pertinent endogenous and exogenous variables and to describe the cause-and-effect *relationships* among them accurately.

Many simulations involve random, or stochastic, variables. Models that have no stochastic components are called deterministic models. If there are stochastic variables, assumptions must be made about the probability distribution or known probability distributions must be included. "Random" numbers must be generated. This can be done by using a table of random numbers or by using computer subroutines to have the computer generate "pseudorandom" numbers. (A more complete discussion of random numbers and stochastic variables is found in the next section in this chapter.)

It usually is impractical to include all possible variables in the model; the simulation developers must decide which are pertinent and attempt to include those variables that reproduce the important features of the real system. They must remember that their task is to represent reality, but they cannot reproduce it. A balance must be reached so that the model is not overly complicated. This is particularly relevant in developing a computer simulation. The computer must be *told everything that it needs to know* in order to generate what the users need to know. All variables must be described precisely, but the complexity of the model affects the amount and difficulty of programming, the computing time, and the validity of the model. It is important to keep the objectives of the simulation in mind.

Estimating Initial Conditions for Computer-Simulated Models

A first step is to estimate the numerical values of the constants and initial values for the parameters of the model and its exogenous variables. These values should provide reliable statistical estimates describing relevant features of the actual system. If the simulation is dynamic—or time-dependent—the program developers also must assign an initial time to the values of variables in the model (e.g., the end of the last full fiscal year or the present time). The sensitivity of the model to each of the initial conditions should be evaluated by comparing corresponding simulations in which distinct values are individually chosen for the initial parameters.

Creating a Computer Program

To develop a computer simulation, the equations must be put into computer-coded form, that is, a computer program must be developed. The algorithm (the set of rules for solving the problem in a logical sequence and a finite number of steps) to be followed by the computer in generating the sequence of values of the endogenous variables is described by a flow chart or flow diagram. The solution values of the endogenous variables are obtained by combining—as specified by the equations of the model and the algorithm—the assumed values of the exogenous variables with stochastic disturbance terms (Adelman, 1972).

A computer simulation can be programmed in a general computer language or in a simulation language. Simulation languages require less programming time but are less flexible than general languages. Simulation languages also have error-checking techniques. But general languages are more flexible in terms of the output reports that can be generated. In addition to the computer and simulation languages listed in the "History" portion of the previous chapter, specialized computer languages have been developed for particular applications (e.g., SIMULATE for economic models; DYNAMO for industrial dynamics and management decision making in a dynamic organizational environment); and languages that permit a digital computer to simulate an analog computer, such as CSMP, CSML, MIMIC, SIMIC, SSSL, DSL/90, and MIDAS. List-processing languages such as IPL-V, LISP, SLIP, and COMIT do not have flow or timing capability. These languages generally are used for nonbehavioral processes (Guetzkow, Kotler, & Schultz, 1972).

Because of their heuristic nature, models to be used in training do not have to be as complete, complex, or exact as those for actual business-decision simulations. However, they should be relatively complete and accurate. The amount of time required to create the program depends on the complexity of the model, the amount of data, etc. It can range from a few days to several months or years.

Testing and Retesting the Program

Next, the program must be tested repeatedly to see if the assumptions on which the model is based are valid, if it is an accurate representation of the real system. The computed solutions of the model equations must be realistic; that is, the model must be able to predict the behavior of the real system. The program is adjusted until the simulation acts like the system being modeled. This process can be very complicated and complex. One method of checking program output is the use of historical data or predictive forecasting under different combinations of controllable conditions, i.e., (a) analysis of variance (the distribution of computer-generated output compared to corresponding historical data); (b) a chi-square test (same frequency distribution between computer-generated data and historical data); (c) factor analysis (on computer-generated dynamics and real system dynamics); and other methods.

The simulation may have to be run numerous times over stipulated time scales. For example, it could be run fifty times, each simulating sixteen fiscal quarters or four years.

Random Numbers, Stochastic Variables, and The Monte Carlo Method

When designing a simulation that models a social, administrative, or economic system, one must take into consideration the random variables over which the users of the actual system have little or no control. These random (or stochastic) variables must be included in the model if the simulation is to be used to make inferences about the behavior of the real system. In most simulations used for human resource development, the element of chance is introduced by the inclusion of human decisions and/or random numbers. Deterministic simulations do not include random fluctuations and, thus, have no stochastic variables.

The fluctuating variables in the simulation are characterized by a probability distribution. "Random numbers are associated with a set of data in order to select a random value from the data" (Jones, 1972). They can be generated by using a table of random numbers or by having the computer generate them (in the latter case, they are actually "pseudorandom" numbers, but in most applications, they function equally well).

Including stochastic variables in a simulation by using pseudorandom numbers is generally referred to as "the Monte Carlo method" (a reference to the roulette wheel or dice used in gambling). Although this terminology is not always technically correct, it is widely used. The Monte Carlo method generally is used in applications in which the system is in equilibrium. There also are dynamic simulations that are used to look at time-dependent variables. These techniques allow the inclusion of a statistically distributed range of values, that is, they take a *sample* from the possible outcomes. Because this technology is so complex, we will not discuss how it is actually done in this book; however, the HRD practitioner who wishes to have a simulation developed (or who has a client who has requested one) would do well to keep these technical considerations in mind.

A simulation also can be used to evaluate risk. In a business application, for example, one could use a simulation to to do a risk analysis of various courses of action in deciding how to expend capital. One could try out the best and worst possibilities by adding the risk factor in calculating possible return on investment. Random numbers can be used to calculate a large number of possible values with associated probabilities. The interrelationships of the factors considered (e.g., money invested, production volume, product price, operating costs, market share) and cause-and-effect relationships such as the value of the dollar, market growth, etc., must be included. One would then test for the range of probabilities.

Other simulation subroutines can be programmed to cover things such as depreciation, return on investment, given cash flow, special tabulations, written reports, graphs, and so on. These can be changed and run more than once. One can use the same basic program and vary the subroutines to work with different aspects of the business or model.

The Decision Tree

If one is not using a computer, one can draw a decision tree to help to identify alternatives and their possible outcomes. This is a graphic representation of choices that is roughly analogous to diagraming a sentence or constructing a mathematical equation. It provides a way to look at and explore possibilities. Both quantitative (financial or objective) and qualitative (emotional or subjective) choices can be evaluated in this manner (Jones, 1972). The following is a simplified example of a decision tree that might be used at University Associates.

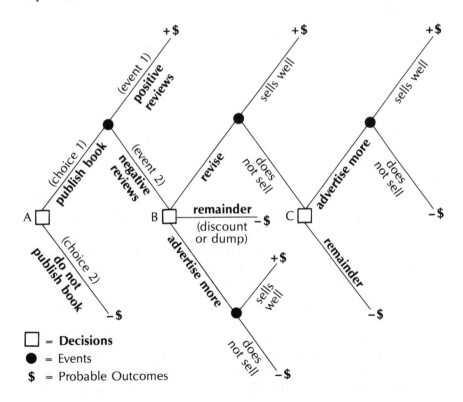

Sample Decision Tree

Note that the possible decisions are represented in a branching mode, i.e., there are points at which one of two or more decisions could be selected, and for each possible decision there are potential positive and negative effects. Numerical values such as percentage probabilities, estimated costs, possible profits and losses, etc., can be added to the decision tree, as can other factors such as people and risk (Jones, 1972).

The Differences Between Simulations and Games

As we have said previously, a simulation is not always a game. A simulation is a representation of one system by means of another system that behaves similarly to the original. The simulation usually is less complex than the original, which makes it easier to analyze and manipulate. Simulations can be used for tactical and exploratory purposes.

One basic definition of a game is that the simulation or model is not rigid in terms of its structure and rules; it can be manipulated by the players (Shubik, 1975). Most experts agree that the distinction between a simulation and a game is that the latter includes the element of human interaction as well as the necessary structure that defines how the game is to be played. Furthermore, not all games are simulations (Greenblat & Duke, 1981). Some games are more free-form and do not involve the use of precise models. Some present a scenario and then let the players take over. Some are really structured experiences or experiments.

The purpose of a game is to involve the players in the operation. The system and/or environment in a game need not be a model of an actual one; it can be a composite or a totally fictitious one that is similar to those encountered in real life. It need not contain all the data or variables encountered in the real world; only those factors that are needed to provide the learning or practice needed and to affect the play and the outcomes are required. In many games, the players have roles.

Like case studies, games are used widely for training. In business and management education, simulation games provide an opportunity for participants to test a variety of techniques and theories. Participants can use different methods of analysis and compare them. They can learn how to apply specific theories and techniques in analyzing information and making decisions. They also learn about the interdependence of functions because the game requires them to work with and through other people in order to accomplish their objectives. This teaches them about communication patterns, consensus, influence, conflict management, and other aspects of group dynamics. A simulation game allows the participants to try again; this increases creativity because the risk is far less than it would be in the real world.

How Games Differ from Case Studies and Role Plays

Because they require more interaction, decision making, and immediate feedback, games tend to be more involving and more realistic than case studies. Typically, case studies are used to focus on interpersonal issues, whereas games are used more to focus on economic considerations, strategies, and plans. Gaming helps the participants to learn about a particular type of *system*: how it functions and operates and how to function effectively in it.

While the feedback in role playing is primarily to create empathy with the role players, the feedback in gaming is to make the consequences of certain decisions or strategies explicit. Gaming also includes an element of risk and uncertainty that is not present in case studies or role playing, especially if the game is based on a simulation that has random or stochastic terms.

6

A Background for Using Games in Human Resource Development

What Simulation Games Are

Games are based on models or simulations that relate to the field in which the particiants are learners. Game models can be analog (verbal, graphic, or physical), mathematical, or digital (computer programs). In pure computer simulations, the computer makes decisions and takes actions; such simulations are not used in gaming. In computerized simulation *games,* the participants *interact* with the computer. They make decisions, enter data and changes in the computer, and receive computerized feedback on the results of their actions.

In most games, the players have *roles*, such as vice president of marketing or controller. These roles may be played by individuals or teams. They may be equal or unequal, specific or general, rigid or flexible, complex or simple, etc. Most games also begin with a *scenario* that describes the system in which the roles and tasks are to occur and states the task to be done or problem to be solved. Some information is general to the system and some pertains to specific roles. Other information, in the form of charts, diagrams, financial statements, market or competitor analyses, other types of reports, statistics, models, and so on, is generally included in the game. In some cases, this information is provided to players, but in others they have to ask for (perhaps even search for) the information they need.

In the typical simulation game, the participants are presented with a business situation and a *task or problem* that they must achieve or solve in a defined period of time. Some games are designed to be run in an hour or more; others may take several days. It is the participants' job to discern and analyze the significant factors in the situation. Many are based on economic models. In the typical business game, the participants must consider numerous organizational, economic, and market factors. In computerized games that have incomplete data, the participants must search for the information that they need. Many contain uncertain conditions, a reflection of real-life markets and circumstances. Management games may involve personnel and resource problems as well as economics.

The participants generally work in *teams* (which may represent departments of the same organization or, more often, separate but equal organizations). The participants must gather data and analyze it, using relevant management or business skills. They must examine relationships among a host of variables, test assumptions, and explore options. They must consider the various effects of different decisions (choices and actions) and identify alternatives. In most cases, this involves studying components of the system (functional analysis) and doing functional planning as well as system planning. The purpose of many business games is to train decision makers to *think strategically,* so each participant team is required to develop a strategy, decide on the actions to be taken, and implement those actions.

An "accounting" system that is built into the game records the players' choices and actions and their consequences as they occur. In a computerized game, this system also monitors the effect on and updates the scenario. Depending on how choices and plays are entered, it may also track what each role (player) does. Complex computer games have not only economic and structural information about the system but also built-in assumptions about behavior and responses. Financial statements and other data that provide *feedback on the consequences of the various actions* are generated. This allows the participants to see cause-and-effect relationships and to identify and discuss what might have been done differently. It provides the participants with a simulated business experience.

A majority of the instructional games used today are in the area of business (management, economics, planning, etc.). In learning about a business or profession, it is necessary to have both an overview—a sense of the whole—as well as an understanding of the components, the functional areas. Both aspects are necessary in order to achieve a perspective. Most organizations today are too large and too complex to permit managers or others to gain direct experience in their many components. Gaming provides a way to obtain a sense of how the components operate and how they affect the total system and vice versa. In order to do this, the games are pared down to relevant aspects of the organization or system; they are not what is termed "environmentally rich." Data are edited and succinct, and extraneous details are omitted. *Time is compressed* so that the decisions that the participants make in a few hours or several days simulate the operation of the modeled organization or department over several months or years. Thus, a game does not present the total reality of the organization or system, but a functional model or simulation of it.

The games that we will discuss in this book are those designed to facilitate specific learning goals; they are not designed for research or for fun. They can be used for a variety of educational purposes, including learning how to deal with models and simulations, learning specific business principles or techniques, learning how to explore and analyze data before making decisions, learning about decision-making processes in groups or organizations, or studying specific data related to a particular field or organization. All involve some skill practice. All have similar components: players, roles, goals, activities or tasks, constraints, rules, and payoffs or consequences (McKenny, 1967).

Many games used in training are analog or mathematical and do not involve the use of a computer. These games tend to be less complex and less expensive. They often are used to illustrate specific problems, skills, or functional areas. Examples of these are board games (e.g., Paul Hersey's *Situational Leadership Simulator®*) and games in which the participants are given oral and written information and perform calculations by hand or calculator without using a computer. In these games, the facilitator explains the procedures of play and the rules and provides the feedback. (In computerized games, these functions—including the functions of empire and referee—are built into the program.) In-basket activities are a simple type of simulation game. These tend to be less structured and more environmenally rich than computerized games. Computerized games, on the other hand, tend to be more expensive and complex, but they offer some possibilities that the others do not. In computerized games, for example, the rules are more enforceable because they are programmed in a cause-and-effect manner.

In all games, the tasks and problems should provide insight into real-life situations. In many cases, they are related to concepts and theories that have been or will be presented in the rest of the training. Although training games may be enjoyable and rewarding for the participants in the long run, they should not be "fun"; in fact, they should be "work." Their purpose is to develop awareness, to stimulate discussion, to build or enhance particular skills, and to aid participants in applying what they have learned.

A Rationale for Using Games

One reason for the popularity of gaming as a training technology is that we all know *how* to learn from games (from our childhoods), even if we are not aware of it. Playing house, playing soldier, and so on, are ways in which children use games to explore and prepare for the real world. As adults in business and society, we still refer to ourselves as "playing the game," "playing by the rules," "dealing with a straight deck," and engaging in "teamwork." Games are perceived as nonthreatening ways in which to interact with others in order to attain common goals. For this reason, they are well suited to training adults in professional skills that require interaction and cooperation with others.

One of the advantages of gaming is that participants tend to feel responsible for the outcome of their team's work. They are drawn into both their roles and their team or organization's goals. As they are drawn into the "work" of the game, they tend to behave naturally, as they would in real-life situations. Feedback that is timely and specific helps them to improve their performance, and they generally do better in each succeeding round. The more "real" the game is to the participants, the more they are concerned with making sound decisions, not figuring out the game in order to "win."

Because there are no "right" answers, no formulas, the focus is on the process as much as on the result. Gaming provides an opportunity for participants to apply and test what they have learned so far and to gain confidence in their ability to organize and analyze data, evaluate and make decisions, and work with others. It increases their understanding of different business functions and of the relationships between parts of a system and the system and its environment.

While learning the specifics of the simulation task, participants also can be exposed to new insights about team functioning: the need to work with and through others, the value of synergy in group decision making, the role of the team leader, the roles of members, the effects of collaboration and competition, and so on.

In addition, the interpersonal dynamics of the game allow the participants to learn something about themselves and how they work with other people. As they hear descriptions of their behavior during the debriefing sessions, they begin to realize the impact of that behavior on others. They have the opportunity to explore patterns that may be interfering with their effectiveness in their real-life work situations. They also can learn from the insights that other participants have. People who one sees as different or difficult to understand can become more real during the debriefing, thus allowing each participant to deal more effectively with different types of people in the future. Participants also can receive positive feedback about their working styles, which can reinforce and help them to "fine tune" effective behaviors.

Gaming can be used to acquaint participants with a wide variety of content areas and skills. These range from general behavioral skills to specialized applications in various types of organizations.

The History of Simulation Games

Adult "games" have been used for centuries by military forces to practice strategies and to train personnel while providing direct feedback on the effects of decisions and actions. The games of Chess, Shogi, and Go were developed from war games used in India, China, and Japan thousands of years ago. Chess was used as the model for war games in Germany in the 1600s and 1700s. It was not until 1798, in Schleswig, that the New Kriegspeil war game employed the use of maps rather than game boards. Even so, the technology of war gaming was not used in the United States until the late 1800s. Once its potential was recognized, however, war gaming was used extensively, and development accelerated. From 1946 to 1956, the Rand Logistics Systems Laboratory, RAND Corporation, and other military contractors developed games to test military strategies. Later, the RAND Corporation developed games for use by the diplomatic corps and business as well as the military.

In 1956, the American Management Association developed a "Top Management Decision Simulation"—the first business management game. It was a general management game, a model of a total organization with a single product in a single market. Teams of participants interacted and competed in making top-management decisions. In the late 1950s and early 1960s, several more games were developed. UCLA first developed an *economic* simulation game in a business context, the UCLA Executive Decision Game. This was used from 1956 on. The second version of the UCLA model was used in other colleges and universities, including the Harvard Business School, Tulane, and Carnegie Tech. In 1959, with expanded computer facilities, UCLA developed a third model that contained information about competitive markets and economic forecasting for industry. This was first used in several schools in Southern California, then by the Harvard Business School in 1961. Schrieber created a "Top Management Decision Game" at the University of Washington in 1959.

Another game was developed at Carnegie Tech and used there and elsewhere. The Carnegie Tech Management Game presented an industrial case, much like the case method, with a great deal of background information. It was based on the premise that business functions are interdependent and that many business decisions require the cooperation of several individuals, even though there frequently are serious time pressures. It was designed to increase the participants' abilities to find, organize, and utilize information from a complex environment, as well as their abilities to forecast economic and other conditions and make plans. At Carnegie and other institutions, graduate students built all or part of the models for these games. This provided them with experience and also saved money (Shubik, 1975).

Games also were being developed by private enterprise, to train managers in specific types of organizations (a specific industry or product such as banking, hotel supply, etc.) or to allow practice in specific functional areas of an organization, such as marketing, accounting, or production. Some games even focused on specific subparts of particular industries. The skills involved in such games were more specialized, less generalized. Many of the simpler functional games were designed for functional managers or experts, not for top management. These games had less emphasis on conceptual problems and more emphasis on techniques. They generally were less complex and required less time to run than the university games. Some of the most important organizational games included IBM's Management Decision-Making Laboratory and Financial, Allocation and Marketing Executive (FAME) Game, developed in 1961, which was used in the IBM Management Training Program. Manufacturing, marketing, and financial decisions were required on three different "decision levels" ranging from simple to complex. This was similar to the Carnegie Tech and Harvard Business School games in some ways, but was rather rigid. Another noteworthy business game was the General Electric Planning Simulation Exercise, IN-TOP (International Operations Simulation), developed in 1963. It simulated management in a multinational corporation and, although very complex, allowed for negotiation. It was faster than the Carnegie Tech game or IBMs' FAME but was more complex and slower than the UCLA and Yale games.

During this period of time, the UCLA game was being studied at the Harvard Business School. This resulted in The Harvard Business School's Management Game, which was used in its MBA program in 1962-63. The students worked in small groups, called "firms." This model was expanded and refined, and a new model was developed late in 1963. Simulation games were used by the Harvard Business School in both its MBA Program and Advanced Management Program to teach skills in areas such as administration, business operations, marketing, planning, auditing, and so on. This model simulated a manufacturer of consumer goods and included the *economic* areas of manufacturing, finance, and sales and marketing. The Harvard game was less behaviorally based than the Carnegie game and more complex than the UCLA game. It was revised in 1966 at which time classes became "corporations," with divisions, officers, and so on. In 1972 it was revised and expanded again, becoming the Harvard Management Simulation Two. The Yale

Macroeconomics Game, designed for both teaching and research, was developed in 1967.

A number of computer models of personality—some designed for psychological experiments—also were developed in the 1960s. Gullahorn and Gullahorn developed a computer model of a social person, HOMUNCULUS, in the early 1960s (Guetzkow, Kotler, & Schultz, 1972). This model involved an exchange of behavior as well as commodities (rewards and costs). It simulated how people make behavioral decisions in interactions with others. These included an "attitude structure" (concepts and beliefs), containing cognitive, evaluative, and emotional components. It was simulated by a complex structure of data in array or list form. "Personality processes" were represented by computer-program subroutines. These generated behavioral or verbal outputs in response to inputs; they contained adjustable parameters that represented personality traits so that personality traits could affect attitude structures. Used first for research in psychiatry, psychology, and psychotherapy, the emerging psychological models soon were adopted by other areas of applied behavioral science, including the diplomatic corps, those who studied international relations, and the military.

Two successful training simulations developed in the late '70s and early '80s were Looking Glass (McCall & Lombardo, 1979, 1982) and the FSI (Financial Services Industry), developed in 1982-1984 at the Graduate School of Business Administration, New York University. Looking Glass, developed from 1976-1979 at the Center for Creative Leadership, simulates a glass-manufacturing corporation. The simulation includes financial, production, and other pertinent business data. The participants are assigned the roles of managers in the company and carry out their assignments in a simulated office setting that includes desks, reports, in-boxes, interoffice mail, telephones, etc. The participants must deal with many different types of communications and problems in a six-hour period that corresponds to a typical business day. The processing of the activity takes another day. Feedback is generated by the participants themselves, by the facilitation staff, and through the use of instruments. The participants thereby have an opportunity to examine not only their general business performance, but also their communications, decision-making processes, personal impact, and a host of related issues.

The use of the computer (particularly the digital computer) has increased the application of simulations and gaming. The computer allows increased speed, accuracy, and impartiality. It reduces errors in calculation and allows increasingly complex, printed reports. As the technology of computer simulation became more prevalent and computer literacy was developed earlier in the public schools, games were developed for elementary and high school use. Board games such as chess and Monopoly were "computerized," and a whole genre of computerized games was developed purely for entertainment purposes. Computer-aided instruction (CAI) is now an accepted part of the educational repertoire. Programs exist that allow the user to construct a new game with various components.

Games that are based on realistic simulations also can be used for trying out or testing models, processes, decisions, etc. As with the use of pure simulations, this provides valuable information without incurring real-life consequences.

The cost of developing a game for use in HRD ranges from a minimal amount for basic materials to hundreds of thousands of dollars (for complex computerized games). Likewise, a simple game can be constructed in a few days, while a highly complex one can take several years to develop. The latter must be widely used in order to be economical.

Game Structures and Types of Games

Many of the games used for management and business training are based primarily mathematical models (finances and economics), rather than behavioral models. Such games deal with decision making, with actions and stages. These games are more likely to incorporate aspects of "game theory." A model that uses game theory provides well-defined rules describing resources, goals, information available, and actions that players can take. These games have one of three major focuses or structures, as described by Shubik (1975).

1. The "strategic or normal form." These games are relatively simple and have limited detail. They may be matrix games. For example, in a 2 x 2 matrix, two players choose among alternatives for a payoff. These may be zero sum games in

which one player wins an amount equal to what the other loses, or there may be more players and more strategies from which to choose. An example of this is the well-known "Prisoner's Dilemma" (Rapoport & Chammah, 1965). The focus in these games is on the payoff. Because these games are intended to raise issues such as the win/lose versus win/win dilemma, they usually teach by analogy.

2. The "extensive form." In these games, the focus is on information, data, details. Typically, one player does not know what another player is doing, so no one's position is clear. In some variations, this information is known. The players must make a sequence of "moves" or other such decisions. They may choose a variety of strategies, based on the positions and moves of their opponents. In some games, such as the extensive form, players repeat patterns to prove certain points, reinforce learnings, etc. To make these games more challenging and exciting, the element of chance often is introduced. It usually is assumed that the players will not cheat.

3. The "characteristic function form." The focus in these games is on coalitions among the participants. They usually involve bargaining or negotiation. Obviously, such coalitions affect the strategies available to the players. These possibilities are depicted in characteristic function—showing the slow but steady gains to be made by cooperating. There may be an element of competition with other coalitions, or the players merely may be trying to outperform the norm group.

If one begins with the extensive form, one can construct a game of the strategic form; if one has the strategic form, one can construct the characteristic form, *but not vice versa.*

According to Shubik (1975), *game theory* requires the consideration of six important areas: (1) rules, words, and coding; (2) rules, rationality, information, and data-processing ability; (3) payoffs, goals, and motivation; (4) poor environments and rich environments; (5) rationality and concepts of solution; and (6) players (individuals or groups). It is much easier to meet these criteria for mathematical games and games that resemble card games or chess (series of moves) than for games that focus on behavioral interactions. This latter group includes, for example, games that focus on communication, interpersonal skills, and survival skills. These involve different motivations and payoffs. Thus, game theory is *not* the only basis for gaming. To illustrate this difference, the six criteria for game theory are listed below, with discussions of how they may or may not be incorporated into training games.

Rules, words, and coding. It is much easier to develop a mathematical code for a physical move—a change to the model. It is extremely difficult to code behavioral intent—statements that may or may not result in specific action. Verbal acts are not necessarily *moves.*

Rules, information, and data processing ability. A team effort generally is required to carry out the functions in more complex games. This may become confusing or complex because different people may interpret information or rules differently. The players also may have different levels of skill in working with the computer. Game theory requres a rational, logical approach, and this may not always be achieved in a team effort.

Payoffs, goals, and motivation. Players must be motivated to play the game; one of the typical ways in which this is done is to establish a payoff. If the game is not motivating, or if the stakes are not high enough for the participant group, boredom and distraction can result, and the goals of the game then are not likely to be met. Participants want to know "what is in it" for them, and the goals of a particular group of participants may not be the same as those assumed by the game developers, so this consideration, although important, can be difficult.

Poor or rich environments. A game that is too environmentally rich (i.e., has too much background and/or personal data) may provide more information that the participants can assimilate and use. The game developers need to decide what data is useful and then incorporate it so that the participants have an opportuntity to make a similar judgment. Some data may not be included or obtained by the players because of time constraints, and some factors, such as the plans of competitors, cannot be known. In an environmentally rich game, (e.g., one that requires some knowledge of a business or a person's history) the players often need to interpret rules as well as facts. Although an environmentally poor game (e.g., one that is more purely mathematical), is closer to game theory, there still may be behavioral aspects.

Rationality and concepts of solution. This relates to the

second consideration. Although a rational solution is required by game theory, it usually cannot be achieved when human behavior is a factor. This may include behavioral structures within the game or the behaviors of players. A purely rational solution is a purely mathematical or mechanical one.

Players (individuals or groups). Again, this is related to the sesond issue. The more players there are, the more complex the game, rules, interpretations, consequences, and solutions become.

In general, a sophisticated game model will include the following:

- The physical, social, economic, and other pertinent features of the system or organization represented, the social environment for each role (player), interdependencies among players. These are givens and are incorporated into the game structure.

- The pertinent features of the outside environment that affect the system or organization, including its market, the economy, customers or clients, etc. These, too, are givens— they are part of the game.

- Timing and the sequence of play. The simuated time in which the game "occurs" can be greater than, the same as, or less than real time. For example, a round of play may take two hours and may simulate two fiscal years in the simulated organization.

- Set of decisions/actions/changes to be made, such as prices, marketing strategies, production and distribution decisions, policies, personnel changes, etc. Such actions are variables; they are influenced and affected by the players. How they are put into effect is not variable; it is governed by operating procedures (rules) that control the play. (The rules, in themselves, are part of the game structure.) These include particular goals, actions, and the means to win.

- Procedures for roles. These behavioral constraints are built into the game and dictate when and how activities can and are to be performed. They include rules governing the interactions between the system and its environment (what happens if). Such activities can affect base information or the model of the system. In many behavioral and operational games, players are *not* provided with all the rules; they are required to explore in order to find some of the information they need to manipulate the game. In mathematical models, rules are givens.

- Accounting procedures. These govern how information is processed—and through what channels and patterns—to make changes.
- Set of results. These dictate the impact of the decisions on the environment. For example, in business games, these may include formulas for changes in sales figures, market share, costs, profits, and so on.
- Enforcement procedures. These "police" the game; they dictate what happens if a player violates a rule. These also include the umpire/referee functions.

Different types of games call for different degrees of cooperation among the players. In some games the participants function independently; there is little or no interaction between them. These are called *mechanistic* games. Decision making is not centralized and often is achieved through voting. In *noncooperative* games, there still may be little communication among the players, but there generally is competition and conflict of interest. The continuum proceeds, through games that involve negotiation and bargaining, to *cooperative* games, which require the players to communicate and to explore common interests in order to reach their objectives.

7

Evaluating and Selecting Games

The first step in deciding on any training technology is identifying the goal(s) of the training—the learning objectives. Then one can ask what the best ways are to achieve those goals. The use of games is one way to relate the concepts and techniques that are being taught to the real-life environment. For example, a particular management game may be appropriate if one of the training objectives is to make the participants aware of how individual goals and strategies must be considered in light of the goals of the organization (Shubik, 1975). If it is decided that a simulation game would be more effective than, for example, a structured experience, instrument, lecturette, role play, or case study, the next step is to review several possible games in the area that is to be the focus of the learning event. The game to be used must fit in with the rest of the training program. It is definitely preferable for the terms used in the game to be the same as those used in the rest of the training. The game also should be related to the other training technologies that will be used during the course, including any handouts, structured experiences, instruments, lecturettes, audiovisuals, etc. The facilitator must decide what the sequence and flow of the course will be and plan for a balance between cognitive and experiential learning.

The model on which the game is based should also be examined. The instructions should be clear. The participants should be able to understand the game, and it should be doable. Yet it should be interesting and challenging. The model must be realistic. The environment in the model should not be static; like real life, it should incorporate—and require the participants to deal with—change. The model must not be so simple that it allows cheating or allows erratic decisions to be processed, but it should respond to actions that are reasonable, logical, and in accord with the training objectives. It also is important that the participants be able to see cause-and-effect relationships as well as the resuts of their actions (McKenny, 1967). Any reports or forms to be generated should look like real ones.

A Check List for Evaluating Simulation Games

In considering a particular game, one needs to ask several questions. These include the following:

Objectives, Content, Structure

1. What is the stated purpose of the game? What is the name of the game?
2. What social systems and processes does the game simulate?
3. What are the training objectives of the game? In what training context is this game designed to be used?
4. What is the focus of the game (e.g., cooperative decision making, planning, forecasting)?
5. Does the game adequately simulate a relevant situation or organization?
6. Does it suit the expectations and objectives of the participants?
7. What are the motivators and payoffs to participants?
8. Can the game be modified? How easy would this be?

Complexity, Clarity, Knowledge, and Skill Required

9. What particular skills and prior knowledge are required of the participants?
10. Is the game primarily mathematical or verbal? If mathematical, how complex are the procedures?
11. How complicated are the game activities? How difficult are the rules and procedures?
12. Are the instructions clear? Are there printed facilitator and participant instructions for playing the game?
13. Is there a referee/umpire built into program or does the facilitator perform this function?

Physical Requirements, Timing, Costs

14. How many participants are optimal (i.e., how many teams are preferable and how many—minimum and maximum—players are there on a team)?

15. What is the cost to obtain the game and what are the operating costs (including any hidden costs such as additional facilitators, computer time, materials, etc.)?
16. How much space is needed? What type of room will accommodate the game?
17. What equipment is needed?
18. How much time will it take to set up the game, run it, and process it?
19. What is the game-time equivalent of real time (compressed or expanded)?

Overall

20. Do the possible learnings and experience to be gained from the game justify its cost, facilitator preparation and training time, and participant time?
21. All things considered, would the game provide a valuable learning experience that is in accord with the goals of the training?

It is important to remember that most games are designed to generate specific types of thought processes and actions. A game that is designed for one purpose may not be easily adapted to achieve another. It is very important to study the model on which the game is based and/or the construction, sequence, and terminology of the game to see if it actually will achieve the stated objectives. In management training, a game should require the participants to obtain information, analyze it, and make decisions. In the social sciences, games may be used to examine and explore models (Greenblat & Duke, 1981; McKenny, 1967).

Staffing Considerations

Many of the questions in the preceding check list suggest considerations about the staffing of the game. The size of the training group, the number of teams, the structure and complexity of the game, the time required, and other issues (e.g., whether teams will generate reports that must be evaluated by the facilitators) may indicate that additional staff members will be needed to facilitate the game. If this is the case, how many facilitators will be needed? What will each facilitator's *role* be? Are the available staff members *technically* able to manage the game? Is there time available before the training session for the facilitator(s) to actually run the game and discuss it before presenting it to the participants? Because games involve specific rules and procedures, *it is imperative that the faciltators be thoroughly familiar with a game before they attempt to use it with a group.* Even then, a game experience will not be the same with one group as it is with another. Each facilitator must be prepared to answer a variety of operational, procedural, and content questions as the game proceeds.

8

Facilitating Games

Prework

As we have stated previously, a facilitator must have worked through a game before attempting to use it with a group. This means allowing enough time to complete several practice rounds. It is imperative that the facilitator become familiar with the various components of the game and know how the game works, the sequence of decisions in the simulation, and how it responds to the players' actions. This also will give the facilitator an idea of how the participants are likely to respond to the game, what kinds of questions they will ask, and what types of problems they may have. In some games, the facilitator serves as the board of directors of the team organizations and asks questions about the teams' decision-making processes. During many games, the facilitator(s) are called on to check reports from the teams. This must be done carefully and with a full knowledge of the game, the mathematics and variables involved, and the data processing required of the groups. The facilitator also must plan for processing discussions after each round of play.

After becoming familiar with the requirements of the game, the facilitator must create a time schedule. This includes the time needed to complete each step and/or stage of the game and time to regroup after interruptions. Breaks must be scheduled in such a way that they do not disturb the pace or flow of the game.

Materials must be collected and/or prepared. The layout of the room and other physical arrangements must be attended to. These may include separate areas for participants with particular roles in the game. Care should be taken to eliminate distractions such as people walking by the windows, the ringing of telephones, people entering the room, and so on. It is preferable if the facilitator can specify that no nonparticipants will be allowed to observe the game or to enter room while the game is being conducted.

Introducing the Game

The participants must be introduced to the game carefully. They should be told why a game has been selected as a tool for learning (e.g., to simulate real-life conditions without the actual risk, to allow them to collect information that may be difficult or too time-consuming to collect in real life, and to allow them to experience some of the pressures and rewards of working with others in an organizational setting). They should understand certain "givens" about the use of games, such as the fact that the time frames in the game will be condensed versions of real time. They should be told that the game model does not duplicate or recreate a real social system or organization but is designed to provide general experience in dealing with similar types of situations or typical business issues. (This realization helps to avoid nitpicking about specifics if participants run into difficulty during the game.) The participants also should understand that because their experiences during the game are generalizations of what they would encounter is real life, they will not be the same in the next situation or a similar one. Tell the participants that their job is to learn the rules and procedures of the game just as they would learn to operate within any social or organizational structure. They then will have the task of using relevant information in combination with appropriate theories or concepts to plan and make game moves. During this process, they also may learn to be explicit, find information, conduct analyses, discuss and collaborate with others, plan strategies and action steps, use feedback, and explore the concept of teamwork.

The introduction to the game also should include a brief explanation of why this particular game was selected, what its objectives are, and how it is related to other theories, models, or methodologies presented in the overall training design.

Describe the basic structure and operation of the game. Read the rules of the game, list them on newsprint, and distribute them in written form, if appropriate. (It is even better if a manual or guide for participants is provided with the game.) List and define the roles of the players. These include what they will do and under what conditions, with whom, and how it will be done. Talk about the objectives of the game in terms of the expected results. Then walk the participants through the procedures for obtaining information, making moves (entering decisions or changes), generating reports, and so on. This information also should be presented in written form, either as handouts or posters.

It can be helpful to explain that is it natural to feel somewhat intimidated or overwhelmed by the rules and processes at the beginning of the game, but that as the participants get into the actual play, some things will become more obvious. Remind the participants that they can refer to their handouts or the posters and can ask questions as things come up. Finally, assure them that the facilitators have actually gone through the game themselves and that it is doable. At this point, the facilitator must be reassuring but also must communicate enthusiasm for the task at hand.

Conducting the Game

While the participants are playing the game, the role of the facilitator will depend on the nature of game. In some games, the facilitator will be required to serve as referee or umpire. This function uses the game rules to rate the players' responses in order to provide immediate feedback to the players on the consequences of their actions. In most computerized games, this function is built into the program and is performed by the computer. At the very least, the facilitator will be called on to answer questions about rules of play, procedures, next steps, and so on.

In a typical business game, the total group is divided into teams of four or five participants each. Each team represents a separate organization, and the team members are assigned roles within that organization. There often are from four to eight teams (organizations in the same industry or area of service) playing the game at the same time. Each organization is assigned a different set of background data, but all are equal in the marketplace. In effect, some competition usually arises between the teams, even if it is not made explicit in the game.

Each team may be called on to make six to ten sets of decisions. Decisions rounds may be divided into periods of time that simulate fiscal years or quarters (e.g., participants make a series of business decisions representing business operations for a three-month period). For each action item required, each team attempts to come up with a common decision that is acceptable to all its members. This helps to teach consensus-seeking processes and the value of synergy in groups. Each team's decisions are reported to the facilitator, who critiques them and provides prompt feedback, or they are programmed into a computer, which immediately feeds back the business effect of the decisions. If a computer is not being used, the decisions can be entered on a preprinted work sheet—a "Decision Sheet"—on which the team members will record each decision, the action taken, and its results.

The team then pauses for analysis, feedback, and planning. During this post-round processing, the facilitator may need to stress that one of the training objectives is to teach the participants to analyze the facts in a particular situation. The facilitator can remind the participants that, as in real life, no two situations are exactly the same, so they cannot just plug in an answer from a set of patterns. In a sense, gaming teaches how to use what one has within the constraints one has. After processing the round, the team members move back into the enactment to make a new series of business decisions. Each enactment provides an opportunity for them to experiment with new techniques, utilize and apply new information, and learn from the insights and feedback provided by others.

In some games, strategies and consequences will provide the basis of the learning. In others, the teams will be required to generate periodic reports on different aspects of their operations and plans. In business games, these may include cash plans, budgets, sales projections, marketing strategies, loans, sales of stock, and so on. Some games require the facilitator to distribute information or reports at specific times during the play. In other games, the reports generated by participants will be collected and logged in by the facilitator. These reports may need to be checked and returned to the teams, if necessary, for corrections.

The facilitator will have to keep track of the timing, give time warnings, and announce the beginning and end of rounds of play, breaks, etc. Participants may need to be regrouped when they return from breaks. It is the facilitator's job to keep the process going but not to interrupt the players unnecessarily or to interfere with their work.

The facilitator also will want to observe what is happening during the game in order to determine how to improve the game during the next round or session and to prepare for the processing discussion that will follow the game. This includes monitoring the degree and types of competition that arise. It is important that the participants stay focused on the processes involved in the game rather than on winning. For maximum learning, it also is desirable that participation be even among the players. If some people are dominating while others seem to be bored, roles of players, team processes, and/or composition of teams may need to be examined.

Because the participants may be confused and apprehensive at first, they may try to find reasons for their lack of expertise. Many will find fault with the game or the facilitator's instructions. When they begin to understand the rules and become familiar with the procedures, they will focus more on the task and begin to scrutinize information, analyze, discuss options and possible outcomes.

The Strategy Phase

As the game progresses, the facilitator may need to encourage the participants to move from analysis toward developing strategies and action plans. As they carry out their plans, i.e., make game moves, they will receive feedback, either from the game program or from the facilitator. This allows them to examine cause-and-effect relationships, re-evaluate, and improve their strategies. This may be a relatively simple task or a very complex one, depending on the previous knowledge and experience of the participants and the game selected. It usually is advantageous for a team to adopt a strategy and follow it, rather than switching strategies during play.

The facilitator may want to pause before initiating succeeding rounds to examine the players' policies and strategies. At this point, conceptual input related to how the task is accomplished may be very useful. For example, it may be helpful to point out that the practice in working with others in making decisions is a valuable learning experience, no matter what types of decisions are made. Participants may need coaching on *how* decisions typically are made in organizations; their assumptions may be that all such decisions are based on economic and statistical information, while the reality is that a great deal of psychological and operational issues are involved. It is important that this aspect of the decision-making process be examined after each round of play (see "An Example of Group Dynamics in Simulation Gaming" later in this chapter).

At some point, the facilitator may decide that it is advisable to change the way in which the game is played in order to introduce new procedures, new patterns, or new theories to make the game better meet the goals of the session and the group. This may be a simple change, such as the way in which reports are made, or it may introduce a new element, such as negotiation or bargaining across teams. Organizational, environmental, or social/cultural factors also can be made part of the game. Of course, the elements and procedures for any change must be made explicit.

Motivation and Payoffs

Most games involve some type of *payoff* to the players as a motivation to play the game well. The payoff is not the same as the *outcome* of the game. The payoff has extrinsic value (provided by the structure or nature of the game) or intrinsic value (defined by the players). It can be psychological or economic. A player's perception of the payoff can be affected by the role that the player has in the game or by the player's previous attitudes or biases. The players' perception of the payoff affects their motivation, and it may not be perceived the same way by all players. The norms of the group also can affect the players' perceptions of the value of the payoff.

The facilitator needs to become aware of the value of the payoff and the outcome of the game to the players in order to understand the effects of game. The values assumed by the developers of the game or the values of the facilitator may not be the same as those of participants (e.g., candy may be a reward to some and may not be to others). Other types of payoffs are dinner with the group, certificates of completion, learning new skills, being with (communicating with, learning from) other professional people, or some type of actual or simulated monetary reward. The facilitator often can gain insight into the participants' attitudes about this issue simply by asking them what motivated them, why they did what they did, and what their assumptions were.

The structure of the game also can affect the participants' behavior. Whether the game is anonymous or involves face-to-face interaction; whether it calls for individual or team activity; whether it is verbal or nonverbal; whether it involves risk taking and of what type and degree; and what the participants know about their competitors all can affect how they respond to the game. To these reactions, the participants will add their own personal values, biases, and feelings about group activities, risk taking, and competition. Some participants may have a drive to do well in front of their peers or to "win." Some will be disconcerted at the prospect of competing or taking risks, while others who are not ordinarily concerned with winning may become motivated as they get into the game. Some may compete for leadership positions within their teams, while others may respond to particular roles. A few participants may seem to be pitting themselves against the environment rather than competing with other players. Some may have more difficulty than others in understanding or adjusting to the rules and procedures of the game. The facilitator can observe all these dynamics and use them in processing the game, not only in terms of what actually occurs but also in terms of personal values, assumptions, and theories related to competition and collaboration, leadership, motivation, and so on.

Another issue that can affect the participants' behavior is the timing of the game. If people perceive that they are running out of time, they may behave (e.g., attempt to make decisions or carry out actions) in ways that are different from what they would do in other circumstances. It is important to keep this in mind in order to allow enough time for all stages of the game and also to consider this aspect in the processing discussion that follows the game. In some instances, making decisions under pressure may be an important dimension ofthe game. Often it is the ability to respond rationally under extreme pressure that separates the more successful from the less successful in real life.

Discussion and Processing

If the game calls for the participants to take on specific roles (e.g., president, financial officer, advertising director), the feedback sessions can include many of the techniques outlined in the fourth book in this Training Technologies set, *Using Role Plays in Human Resource Development*. For example, individuals within the group can fill out response or reaction sheets that become the basis for analyzing and learning from the process. Sufficient time must be allotted to providing feedback during the stages of the game and to critiquing, discussing, and processing the experience at the end. For example, if the action stage of the game time takes four hours, at least one and one-half hours should be allowed for feedback and processing.

In a typical processing session, the players first will share their reactions to the experience, their feelings about what happened in their groups, etc. When the air has been cleared of affective issues, they can begin to examine the model on which the game is based, the various roles that were involved, and so on. This can lead to a less generalized discussion of the actual roles in their teams, and it may be appropriate to have the participants discuss these issues in their team groups first, then report the highlights of their discussions to the total group. Before these discussions, they can be given discussion guidelines (either verbal guidelines that are reinforced by newsprint posters or preprinted handouts). The group members can compare their observations about what happened during their groups' sessions. These discussions will focus on two levels: a) what was simulated, what happened in terms of the game task, and the results; and b) the interpersonal (e.g., leadership, decision making, problem solving) dynamics in the group.

In the total group session that follows, participants can attempt to draw connections between the interpersonal dynamics and the tasks and structures of the game. It may help to have them create graphic representations. The discussions should be linked to real-world examples and extended to the participants' own work applications. Finally, they should be asked to state what they learned or relearned from the experience and how the details of the game process were different from what they expected. Above all, it is important to link the outcomes of the processing discussion to the objectives stated at the beginning of the game training.

An Example of Group Dynamics in Simulation Gaming

Wagner (1965) describes the use of the UCLA Executive Decision Game 2 as an example of the group dynamics that might emerge in conducting a simulation game. This game simulates the operations of a multifirm, one-product industry; its purpose is to help managers and students of management learn more about top-level business planning and policy formulation. One day of play simulates more than five years of "experience." In some ways it is similar to a case study. Each team plays the top management of a different firm and makes decisions for a "fiscal quarter" on issues such as price of product, production volume, advertising budget, research and development budget, investment in plant and equipment, dividends, etc. The decisions are entered into a computer, along with data summarizing the conditions of the firms at the end of the preceding quarter. The computer simulates the quarter's operations and prints out the following reports for each firm: sales volume, percent share of industry sales, current inventory quantity, production capacity for the next quarter, profit and loss, receipts and disbursements, and financial condition. The task of the players (managers) is to balance the controllable factors in order to make the most of available resources and potential. Efforts to increase sales must be related to costs in terms of reduced margins and enlarged budgets and phased with changes in plant capacity and production volume. Investment programs and dividend policies must be geared to profits and to available funds. All these factors must be balanced in the face of continually changing competitive and general economic conditions. The need for planning is emphasized by the fact that relatively stable policies are more effective than policies involving much fluctuation. The instructions also discuss the market, operating costs, plant expansion, finances, and goals.

In the group studied, after each decision-making period, each team analyzed its decision process, focusing primarily on interpersonal relations and group behavior as they affected business tasks. After the decision-making phase, but before the analysis, each participant was asked to complete a rating scale with four questions:

1. How adequate were the team's procedures for making this decision?
2. To what extent did I help or hinder the contributions of others to the decision?
3. To what extent did I feel helped or hindered by others in contributing my ideas to the decision?
4. How do I feel about my group?

The groups that Wagner studied evidenced three stages of behavior during three rounds of decision-making processes. The first involved *competitive* interpersonal behaviors. When this was processed (after some resistance) and the dynamics were understood, they began to overcompensate. In the second phase, some task accomplishment was sacrificed because of the heavy investment in *maintaining group harmony at all costs.* After processing this, the groups were able to move to a more *balanced* team effort that involved realistic problem solving. The disruptive behavior of the first session could be attributed to the players' lack of familiarity with business games. No specific criteria were stated regarding success in the game, so it was impossible to compare the stages of decision making with the quality of the business decisions.

The major learning here is that process analysis was needed to help the groups to make the transition to a team approach. Of course, the maturity of the group members will affect the level of decision-making processes attained. But groups should improve in consecutive plays if there is adequate processing in between.

Using Simulations to Teach Strategic Planning

Changing social and economic environments, rapid technological advances, competition, and other factors make it necessary for most organizations to engage in strategic planning. In this process, the leaders of the organization must analyze how each part of the organization will contribute and how each will affect the others. They must identify alternatives in financial management, investments, production, services, physical operations, warehousing and distribution, sales and marketing, personnel, and so on. Typically this process calls for them to establish objectives and goals for the organization and to factor in possible strategies by competitors, possible economic conditions, trade restrictions, resources, etc., and to develop long-range plans and contingency plans that create a balance between the different divisions or departments within the organization. According to Pfeiffer, Goodstein, and Nolan (1986), each organization needs to go through this process annually. One of the best ways to make such decisions is to use a computerized model of the organization to test various types of data and to evaluate different strategies (Jones, 1972). Computerized gaming is an excellent way to teach managers the "hands-on" part of strategic planning. They can practice inputting data, doing calculations, and producing written reports.

9

Considerations in Developing Simulation Games

By now, it should be clear that each different game has its own procedures, rules, constraints, and so on, so no actual formula applies for creating a game. We have tried to point out that any game (particularly a computerized game) may involve a complex simulation with mathematical, statistical, and programming aspects; therefore, this discussion will not reiterate how to develop a simulation but will focus on what the HRD practitioner needs to know in helping others to develop a game for training purposes.

Purpose and Use

The initial consideration, of course, is the purpose of using the game. What are the training objectives? Who has requested that the game be developed, i.e., who is the client? Why would a game be preferable to some other training technology? Then, what are the objectives of the game itself, i.e., what is it to teach or achieve? Will the game involve competition? What types of decisions will be made? Who are the players: are they male and/or female?; what are their ages?; what is their level of education?; what are their professions? Will the group be heterogeneous or homogeneous? What previous experience do the participants have with gaming? What are their motives for playing the game? What size of group typically will play the game? Will decisions and game moves be made by individuals or by teams? It is preferable if the game design can take into account the level of sophistication of the possible participant group and allow for differences in individual capacities and decision-making styles.

The second set of questions involves the use of the game: where, how, and when it will be used. Will it be used primarily for training adult professionals or might it also be used in a university, college, or high school classroom? Is it part of a series or will it be used by itself? What, if any, follow-up is required?

The Simulation Model

Next, the designers must determine the type of model or simulation to be used. Most games are a combination of more than one type, although one may be predominant. The focus of the game also will help to determine the vehicle: will the participants be concerned with allocating scarce resources; will they focus on interpersonal relationships and group dynamics; or will they be learning about the interrelationships between the parts of a complex system? The focus of the game may well indicate the media to be used. This determination, in turn, will indicate the type of instructions to be given and, if appropriate, the computer language to be used and the type of program to be developed.

The simulation model then must be developed, including background data (historic, cultural, geographic, etc.) and the current situation (the scenario), data about environmental and other forces (variables), and the symbolic structure and procedures (the mechanisms of the play, how the game proceeds). These include structures and procedures for communicating, for obtaining information, for bargaining, for indicating moves, and for evaluating moves and generating results. They must be framed in game-specific language. This is the step in which a conceptual map of the game, a flow chart, is developed.

In representing the system and the sets of interactions within it, one must make decisions about what is and is not to be included. The major components include a set of roles, the scenario, and a set of accounts (how decisions affect results and how results affect the status of players and modify the data set) (Greenblat & Duke, 1981). If the roles of players are very strong and the scenario and accounting procedures are weak, the game is, in effect a role play. This may be most effective for studying certain interpersonal dynamics. If the scenario is the strongest element, the game will resemble a case study, which may be helpful in analyzing data and making certain types of decisions. A more pure simulation will contain a stronger set of accounts. This would be required for games in which financial and other types of decisions will affect structures and numerical data.

In designing the game, one must keep the conceptual map in mind at all times. This process may be somewhat analogous to writing a novel in which the characters, their relationships, and the times and dates of events must be consistent throughout. In a game, the components are the system, its pertinent components and characteristics, roles, linkages among components and roles, and the themes, issues, or problems to be highlighted.

Stylistic and Functional Issues

Given these determinations, the designers then will be called on to make a number of stylistic and functional decisions that are not part of the basic model. These are the elements that make a game different from a simulation. They include the type or format of the game itself; how it will be staged; the degree of relation to reality; the level of abstraction; whether the message to the players will be implicit or explicit; how the players will access information; the format for providing information; the simulated versus real time frames; which structures will be predetermined and which, if any, will be generated by the players; how elements such as power and resources will be represented; whether bargaining or coalitions will be permitted; whether there will be an emphasis on cooperating or on winning; how rounds of play will be structured; whether cycles will be repeated and whether they will become more complex; the steps and tasks involved in the play; whether there will be any penalties for failure; whether reports will be issued to players (and, if so, how and in what form); whether the players will be required to prepare reports (and, if so, in what form, how, and when); whether breaks or intermissions will be written into the game; and so on. The designers must consider the possible players in determining how the game and its procedures will be presented to them, what processes will be used to teach them how to play the game, and how much time will be required for them to learn it. For a training game, the designers will want to achieve a balance between intense involvement (emotional and physical) and cognitive processes (analytical and intellectual). They also must decide what the balance will be between player ability and the element of chance.

In general, the object of training games is to have the participants consider the information they have, search for new information, discuss things, make choices, receive feedback on the results of those choices, and clarify their understanding of what occurred. It is best if there are at least two or three players involved in making every important decision, and five seems to be optimal. If there are only two players on a team, one is likely to dominate the other. However, if there are more than five, the decision-making and discussion processes can become endless.

In some games, the scenario is presented to the participants at the beginning of the game, but additional information also is inserted at strategic times during the play to change the nature of the problem, to increase time pressures, or to change the dynamics in some other way. Information to the players in a game that simulates an organization can be in the same forms as information to the participants in a structured experience or in-basket activity. This information can be part of the game package or can be prepared by the facilitator prior to the game. In most cases, it will be in a form that simulates letters, memoranda, notes, announcements, agendas, minutes of meetings, calendars, telephone logs, other written reports, and newspaper or magazine articles.

Two related elements of game design that must not be overlooked are the police and umpire/referee functions. The first enforces the procedures, the rules, and specifies what will happen when procedural rules are broken. The second establishes mediation procedures to resolve impasses and disputes. As we have said before, these functions can be built into a computer program or they can be performed by the facilitator.

The rules of the game must state clearly and specifically what procedures are incorporated into the game or allowed and how they are to take place. If several teams are to be engaged, separate scenarios must be developed for each team. There also must be clear instructions about how players can influence or modify the structure of the game.

Some game designers include suggested procedures for debriefing the game. Because the discussion and processing stages after rounds and after the completion of the game are so important, these suggestions and guidelines can be extremely helpful. They are much like the "notes for the facilitator" found in structured experiences, role plays, and case studies. They can help the facilitators to prepare for the types of reactions and questions that the participants may generate and also can help them to relate the game experience and learnings to the real world in order to help the participants to formulate back-home applications.

Constructing and Testing the Game: Time and Money

Once the designers have decided what the game will include, it must be constructed, that is, a vehicle (e.g., boards, pieces, cards, models, etc.) must be created through which participants will play the game. If game is to be computerized, the program must be written, the data must be loaded, calibrated, and tested.

The scope of the game will be dictated by the training objectives but, in reality, it is limited only by the time and resources available and by what is programmed into it. In the long run, gaming can be expensive. The costs include the time and expense of building and testing the model, reproducing it, implementing the system (training operators, computer programming, etc.), running the game to test all aspects of it, and redesigning the game as necessary. To be valid, the testing would require numerous (some say as many as ten) runs. The first tests typically are with the families and friends of the game developers. The game is revised as indicated, and the second series of tests typically are with colleagues of the developers or the types of people who would use the game (i.e., facilitators and instructors). Further revisions are made as required, and then the game is tested with participants who are aware that the game is in a developmental stage. These players evaluate the game from the player's point of view. Obviously, the development and testing of a game can consume a great deal of time. In addition to human time, one must include computer time and/or time to develop or collect game materials and other supplies. In implementing the game, again there are the expenses of facilitator time (evaluation, preparation, and running the game), physical accommodations, materials and supplies, and participant time.

In determining whether to develop a game, then, one must consider the financial aspects as well as whether one has "a good idea." Are there adequate resources (time, money, personnel) to support the design, construction, and testing phases? Has allowance been made for redesigning and retesting? What will be the costs to reproduce the game? One also must consider the marketability of the game. What is the demand for the learnings to be generated by this particular game? What will it cost the user to purchase and run the game? How much time is required to prepare for and conduct the game? How difficult are the materials to understand, manipulate, etc.? Is the game easy to ship, carry, and store? A game that has a narrow application probably would not be economically feasible unless it were simple to produce. A game that is marketable but based on a bad simulation or badly designed could result in anything from chaos to the wrong kind of learning. It is hoped that this book will help to reduce the possiblity of that outcome and to increase the HRD practitioner's skill in evaluating, developing, and using this increasingly popular training technology.

Principal Components of Case Studies, Role Plays, Simulations, and Games

Case Study	Role Play	Simulation	Game
Background data	Background data	System Background data	System Background data
Scenario	Scenario	System scenario	Scenario
	Roles	Endogeneous and Exogenous variables, stochastic variables	Roles
			Variables
			Methodology, accounting procedures
		Methodology, accounting procedures	**Symbolic structure and procedures (rules) of operation**

References and Bibliography

Adelman, I. (1972). Economic system simulations. In H. Guetzkow, P. Kotler, & R.L. Schultz (Eds.), *Simulation in social and administrative science: Overviews and case-examples.* Englewood Cliffs, NJ: Prentice-Hall.

Andrews, E.S., & Noel, J.L. (1986). Adding life to the case-study method. *Training and Development Journal, 40,* 28-29.

Andrews, K.R. (1953). *The case method of teaching human relations and administration.* Cambridge, MA: Harvard University Press.

Barton, R.F. (1970). *A primer on simulation and gaming.* Englewood Cliffs, NJ: Prentice-Hall.

Belch, J. (Ed.) (1974). *Contemporary games: A directory and bibliography describing play situations or simulations (Vol. 1: Directory; Vol. 2: Bibliography).* Detroit, MI: Gale Research.

Boocock, S.S., & Schild, E.O. (1968). *Simulation games in learning.* Beverly Hills, CA: Sage.

Boyd, B.B. (undated). Developing case studies: A six-page method for writing cases to fit special needs. In B.B. Boyd (Ed.), *Supervisory training: Approaches and methods* (pp. 99-108). Alexandria, VA: American Society for Training and Development.

Boyer, R.K. (1987). Developing consultation skills: A simulation approach. In W.B. Reddy & C.C. Henderson, Jr. (Eds.), *Training theory and practice.* Arlington, VA: NTL Institute for Applied Behavioral Science/San Diego, CA: University Associates.

Chartier, M.R. (1981). Facilitating simulation games. In J.E. Jones & J.W. Pfeiffer (Eds.), *The 1981 annual handbook for group facilitators.* San Diego, CA: University Associates.

Dooley, A.R,. & Skinner, W. (1977). Casing casemethod methods. *Academy of Management Review, 2*(2), 277-289.

Duke, R.D., & Greenblat, C.S. (1979). *Game-generating games: A trilogy of games for community and classroom.* Beverly Hills, CA: Sage.

Dukes, R.L., & Seidner, C.J. (Eds.). (1978). *Learning with simulations and games.* Beverly Hills, CA: Sage.

Ford, L. (1970). *Using the case study in teaching and training.* (Multi-Media Teaching & Training Series.) Nashville, TN: Broadman Press.

Frazer, J.R. (1975). *Business decision simulation: A time-sharing approach.* Reston, VA: Reston Publishing Co.

Gordon, R.A., & Howell, J.E. (1959). *Higher eduction for business.* New York: Columbia University Press.

Greenblat, C.S., & Duke, R.D. (1981). *Principles and practices of gaming simulaton: Rationale designs and applications* (rev. ed.). Beverly Hills, CA: Sage.

Guetzkow, H., Kotler, P., & Schultz, R.L. (1972). *Simulation in social and administrative science: Overviews and case-examples.* Englewood Cliffs, NJ: Prentice-Hall.

Gullahorn, J.T., & Gullahorn, J.E. (1972). Social and cultural system simulations. In H. Guetzkow, P. Kotler, & R.L. Schultz (Eds.), *Simulation in social and administrative science: Overviews and case-examples.* Englewood Cliffs, NJ: Prentice-Hall.

Horn, R.E., & Cleaves, A. (1980). *The guide to simulations/games for education and training* (4th ed.). Beverly Hills, CA: Sage.

Inbar, M., & Stoll, C.S. (1972). *Simulation and gaming in social science.* New York: The Free Press.

Jones, G.T. (1972). *Simulation and business decisions.* London: Penguin.

Kaplan, R.E., & Drath, W.H. (1987). Realistic simulation: An alternative vehicle for laboratory education. In W.B. Reddy & C.C. Henderson, Jr. (Eds.), *Training theory and practice.* Arlington, VA: NTL Institute for Applied Behavioral Science/San Diego, CA: University Associates.

Leenders, M.K., & Erskine, J.A. (1973). *Case research: The case writing process.* London, Ontario, Canada: Research & Publications Division, School of Business Administration, The University of Western Ontario.

McCall, M.W., Jr., & Lombardo, M.M. (1979). *Looking Glass, Inc.: The first three years* (Technical report No. 13). Greensboro, NC: Center for Creative Leadership.

McCall, M.W., Jr., & Lombardo, M.M. (1982). Using simulation for leadership and management research: Through the looking glass. *Management Science, 28*(5), 533-549.

McFarlan, F.W., McKenney, J.L., & Seiler, J.A. (1970). *The management game: Simulated decision making.* New York: Macmillan

McKenney, J.L. (1967). *Simulation gaming for management development.* Boston: Division of Research, Graduate School of Business Administration, Harvard University.

Mize, J., & Cox, G. (1968). *Essentials of simulation.* Englewood Cliffs, NJ: Prentice-Hall.

Naylor, T.H. (1970). *Computer simulation experiments.* New York: John Wiley.

Newell, W.T., & Meier, R.C. (1972). Business system simulations. In H. Guetzkow, P. Kotler, & R.L. Schultz (Eds.), *Simulation in social and administrative science: Overviews and case-examples.* Englewood Cliffs, NJ: Prentice-Hall.

Pierson, F.C., et al. (1959). *The education of American businessmen.* New York: McGraw-Hill.

Pigors, P., & Pigors, F. (1961). *Case method in human relations: The incident process.* New York: McGraw-Hill.

Rapoport, A., & Chammah, A.M. (1965). *Prisoner's dilemma.* Ann Arbor, MI: The University of Michigan Press.

Ruben, B.D. (1972). Games and simulations: Materials, sources, and learning concepts. In J.W. Pfeiffer & J.E. Jones (Eds.), *The 1972 annual handbook for group facilitators.* San Diego, CA: University Associates, 1972.

Schmidt, J.W. (1970). *Simulation and analysis of industrial systems.* Homewood, IL: Richard D. Irwin.

Shubik, M. (1975). *Games for society, business, and war: Towards a theory of gaming.* New York: Elsevier.

Starbuck, W.A., & Dutton, J.M. (Eds.). (1970). *Computer simulation in human behavior.* New York: John Wiley.

Stadsklev, R. (1979). *Handbook of simulation gaming in social education (Part 1: Textbook; Part 2: Directory of noncomputer materials)* (2nd ed.). University, AL: Institute of Higher Education Research and Services.

Strunk, W., Jr., & White, E.B. (1979). *The elements of style* (3rd ed.). New York: Macmillan.

Tagiuri, R., Lawrence, P.R., Barnett, R.C., & Dunphy, D. (1968). *Behavioral science concepts in case analysis: The relationship of ideas to management action.* Boston, MA: Division of Research, Graduate School of Business Administration, Harvard University.

Tansey, P. (Ed.). (1971). *Educational aspects of simulation.* London: McGraw-Hill.

Taylor, J., & Walford, R. (1978). *Learning and the simulation game.* Beverly Hills, CA: Sage.

Towl, A.R. (1969). *To study administration by cases.* Boston: Graduate School of Business Administration, Harvard University.

Wagner, A.B. (1965). The use of process analysis in business decision games. *The Journal of Applied Behavioral Science, 1*(4), 387-408.

Willings, D.R. (1968). *How to use the case study in training for decision making.* London: Business Publications.

Yin, R.K. (1983). *The case-study method: An annotated bibliography.* Beverly Hills, CA: Sage.

Appendix 1:
An Article on
Using Simulation Games

Facilitating Simulation Games

Myron R. Chartier

Experiential-learning methods are widely used as major training interventions by human relations facilitators. According to Gaw (1979, p. 147), "experiential learning provides activities that have the potential to involve the whole person in the educational process." As experiential, communication devices, simulations potentially have the ability to convey a gestaltic awareness of a referent reality. Social-simulation games, which involve participants interactively in a simulated environment and create within them an awareness and understanding of social systems, are dynamic, operating models of human realities.

The purpose of this article is to provide the human relations facilitator with an overview of this highly involving technology.

Reprinted from *The 1981 Annual Handbook for Group Facilitators,* John E. Jones & J. William Pfeiffer (Eds.), San Diego, CA: University Associates.

Three aspects are explored: viewing simulation games as simulated social systems, facilitating simulation games, and designing such games. The primary emphasis is on facilitation.

GAMES AS SIMULATED SOCIAL SYSTEMS

Simulations are attempts to simulate social realities (e.g., marital dyads, decision-making groups, organizations, neighborhoods, cities, nations, or groups of nations). Many behavioral scientists view such entities from a social-systems perspective (Katz & Kahn, 1978; Olsen, 1968). Any scientific attempt to understand a social organism as a system involves the observer in theoretical model building. Because of the complexity of social reality, critical variables must be identified and extracted from the whole. Such processes, however, tend to oversimplify social reality in order to make it comprehensible.

Definition of a Social System

A system is a bounded set of components standing in transactive relationship to each other. In a social system the whole is more than the sum of its parts. A simulation seeks to operationalize the trans-active relationships of a social system so that its functions and processes may be observed and experienced. For example, "The Marriage Game" has to be comprehended in terms of two sets of elements: those in the society at large and those in the individuals making marital decisions. This game posits that marital interactions take place between persons who live in a world of external social facts, many of which have been internalized, affecting conceptions and values (Greenblat, 1975).

Primary Components of Social Systems

Simulations seek to place the following primary components of social systems into an actual transactive relationship:

1. *People.* People make a system "social" rather than "mechanical." The ways people or groups of people interact with

respect to the other basic components define the nature of a system with respect to kind (e.g., a family, a classroom, or a decision-making group) and quality (i.e., salubrious or pathogenic).

2. *Goals.* Because goals draw people together for interaction, social systems are purposeful. People develop social systems to accomplish their purposes, but goals vary in different social systems.

3. *Tasks.* To accomplish their goals, people have to perform certain tasks. Each social system has its task requirements, and they vary widely among social organisms.

4. *Structure.* In order to perform task requirements, social structure is necessary. This component is intermeshed with the other six. For example, the nature of the goals, the demands of the tasks, and the characteristics of people have a fundamental influence upon structure.

5. *Resources.* Resources are needed to perform tasks and accomplish goals. These include people and their varied abilities, finances, time, space, and facilities.

6. *Values.* This component varies with the type of social system (e.g., loyalty in families, profit in businesses).

7. *Constraints.* The limits of a social system are defined by its firm (but alterable) constraints. These tenacious forces provide an ordered consistency in social systems.

THE NATURE OF SOCIAL SYSTEMS

Any one component by itself would fail to create a social unit, and changing any one component would redefine the system. The various elements acting upon each other create a social system.

Social systems are open systems—that is, they receive inputs from the environment, process them, and send outputs back to the environment. However, they are also bounded systems, because they have boundaries that filter the inputs and outputs. Social units are in constant transactive relationships with their environments. In that sense they are adaptive; "they possess the ability to react to their environments in a way that is favorable. . .to the continued operation of the system" (Hall & Fagen, 1975, p. 61).

Figure 1 is a verbal-graphic model of a social system. It portrays the various components and their transactive processes in relationship to each other and to the environment.

FACILITATING SIMULATION GAMES

Human relations facilitators who want participants to experience the complexity of a social system with its constant interplay of variables will find simulations a suitable technology. The games are available for the four major areas of activity in human relations—individual, group, organization, and community (Jones & Pfeiffer, 1975)—with a focus on personal growth as well as leadership, organization, and community development (Horn & Cleaves, 1980).

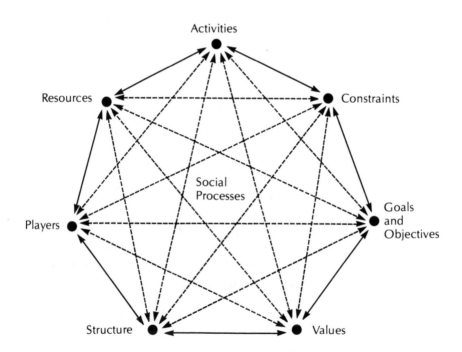

Figure 1. The Social-Systems Model

Evaluating Simulation Games

Most of the game manuals explain the theoretical model and state the principal objectives. After reading the rules and actually playing the game, the facilitator may discover other training values or conclude that the stated objectives have been exaggerated or that important concepts are oversimplified or neglected. The evaluation should also consider the abilities and interests of the potential participants, because simulations vary in subject matter, complexity, and sophistication.

The novice facilitator should use simple games to prevent frustration or disenchantment with games. However, the game must be difficult enough to challenge the participants. The room space and physical equipment required must also be considered. Some evaluation questions are provided in the appendix to this article to help in making decisions about the worth and suitability of a game in relation to training objectives, the abilities of the participants, and needed facilities.

Preparing the Facilitator

The key to a successful game experience is thorough preparation. The facilitator must discover what is being simulated and how the designer is attempting to bring these processes into operation through game play. This information is often included in the instructional materials that accompany the games.

As the facilitator studies the prepared materials, he or she should try to understand the interrelationships among the game components, which parallel the elements within a social-systems model (see Figure 1).

Players

The first component consists of the *players*. Answers to the following questions will provide needed information: Are individuals or teams used? Do the players assume a role as in role-playing games? How should roles be assigned? What is the optimum/minimum number of people who can play the game? Can the game be played by an odd number of players or must the number be even?

Goals and Objectives

The next component includes both *goals* and *objectives* and should provide answers to the following questions: What are the goals of the simulated processes? What educational/training objectives does the game provide for the players? Is the game structured to communicate concepts and their utilization, or is it structured to involve people in new feelings, attitudes, and/or behaviors? The goals and objectives may be the same or quite distinct. Goals may relate to the simulated processes, whereas objectives may be related to training.

Activities

Activities in a simulation game are related to the task requirements of a social system. Relevant questions include the following: In what specific tasks does the game involve players? Is there a sequence of activities? If so, what? Is the game played in cycles? How are the game activities related to the educational/training objectives? What is required from the players? How much time is needed?

Structure

Simulation games and social systems require *structure*, which raises the following questions: What space and furniture arrangements are needed to create the simulated social dynamics? Is more than one room required? If players must move around, how much space is needed? Does the game require individuals or teams in special locations? Will the room accommodate the noise level of the activities?

Resources

The *resources* component consists of the game materials, which can range from sheets of paper (explaining profiles or scenarios for role playing) to game boards, poker chips, chance cards, score sheets, etc. The facilitator needs to know what these materials are and should find answers to the following questions: How are they related to each other? With which rules do they function? How are they related to the game activities? How much time is needed to set up materials for game play? Are there enough materials for the present purposes? What other resources and equipment are needed?

Values

Simulations—like social systems—have *values*. Some game instructions specify values, but others require the facilitator to discern the values by examining the other game components. The values may become apparent after the game is in progress.

Constraints

The *contraints* in a simulation game are its rules and procedures. A detailed study of the game rules will reveal how the game will function as a social system. Failure to understand the game rules and procedures can short-circuit the social dynamics of the entire experience, or even cause them to fail.

After the rules and procedures are understood, the facilitator needs to decide how these will be communicated to the players. Manuals for participants, which are sometimes included with the game, are usually quite brief, because participants are rarely told all the details in advance; they learn the details as they particpate. Some games are marketed with sound filmstrips that give a general overview and brief explanation of the game rules, and others require the facilitator to instruct the players orally or to provide a summary of the rules in print.

Facilitator's Rules

The facilitator must understand his or her *role* in the game, because he or she is responsible for the enactment of a simulated social system through game play. The primary functions of the facilitator are understanding and interpreting game rules, answering players' questions, encouraging participation and experimentation, helping players cope with uncertainty, and helping the participants to discuss and evaluate their experience.

After the game components and the facilitator's role are understood, defects and errors should be removed before the simulation is formally introduced in a training event. Several options are available:

1. Without actually playing a simulation game, a person can acquire a feel for it by playing the various roles and performing the activities.

2. Some simulation games need to be played in advance with several participants. These same participants could be assigned to major roles in the actual simulation or scattered among the teams so that they could help the slower participants.

3. A select number of persons could be assigned the task of learning the rules, introducing the game to a group, and supervising the play. The facilitator would then be free to help participants integrate the game experience with selected training objectives by planning a postgame discussion and related activities.

Any of these options will decrease confusion and increase the positive training experience.

Preparing the Players

After the facilitator is thoroughly prepared, he or she must prepare the players by assigning roles, deciding on the number of players, and introducing the simulation.

Assigning the Roles

In simulations with a role-playing component, there may be little differentiation between roles (for instance, all may play the role of managers) or roles may vary in the degree of activity and aggressiveness required (for example, a small number may play management roles while the rest play workers). In the latter case the problem of casting arises. Casting practices vary from choosing numbers out of a hat to asking for volunteers, assigning roles arbitrarily, or deliberately assigning leadership roles to those who are natural leaders in the group.

Teams for a simulation should be heterogenously grouped rather than homogeneously (Chartier, 1973). Participants' satisfaction with and performance in the game are maximized when competing teams have similar potential in game competition. Team role playing may be useful with slow or easily discouraged participants. Allowing a couple to play a single role decreases frustration at setbacks and provides the security of a teammate for decisions. Team efforts also accommodate more participants and may be especially advantageous with large groups.

Some games can be played more than once so that participants have an opportunity to play different roles and gain a better understanding of the simulated process. When multiple role playing is possible, it needs to be planned and encouraged.

Deciding Number of Players

The facilitator's manual usually indicates an optimum number of players. When groups become too large, participants lose interest, and training effectiveness is decreased because participants learn rules less efficiently, interact less, participate less actively, and make fewer moves (Chartier, 1973). With some games a large group can be divided into several subgroups, each playing separately and using a set of game materials.

Introducing the Game

The introduction will depend partly on the intended use of the game and on the training objectives. The facilitator must communicate two points: First, the participants need to understand the purpose of the game. If they have never played a simulation, the briefing could include a definition of "simulation," a comparison of simulation games with other games (such as charades), and an overview of the content and value of the game. Second, the briefing should include a clear, concise statement of how the game operates. The physical layout and game materials should be discussed. Rules need to be explained and, in some cases, demonstrated. A broad overview of the roles is useful. Knowledge of these factors helps to eliminate uncertainty. Overexplaining, however, will dampen the trainees' enthusiasm. Specific questions can be handled as they arise in the course of play.

The quality of this pregame briefing is likely to affect the participants' predisposition toward the game experience, their enjoyment of the game, and their acquisition of knowledge during the game. The facilitator needs to display enthusiasm and confidence in order to present the learning experience as attractively as possible.

Facilitating the Game

The primary task of the facilitator is to help the simulation function smoothly. He or she should circulate in the room to answer those questions related to the *rules* of the game. The participants should discover for themselves the points of game strategy, the values of game play, and the things to be learned from participation. The facilitator may ask the participants questions unrelated to the game in order to help them arrive at their own solutions. If the facilitator forgets a rule or if a rule is not discussed in the facilitator's manual, one can be created on the spot. If materials become misplaced, the facilitator's improvisation can save the game. Active participation on the part of players should be encouraged. The extent of participation by players is directly related to the degree of learning from and satisfaction with the game experience (Chartier, 1973). The facilitator can be many things—a referee, an enabler, a coordinator, a scorekeeper, a timekeeper, and/or an observer—depending on the game, and must be imaginative and flexible.

Generally, it is unwise for someone to facilitate a game and participate in it at the same time, because facilitators who keep changing their own roles are likely to play the roles partially and poorly. If there is little to do but watch the action of the game, a facilitator may choose to participate as a player. If this is done, however, this person has relinquished the role of facilitator and has turned the control of game flow and the postgame discussion over to the group. There is nothing wrong with this, but one must be clear about what has been done and act accordingly. A person either facilitates the game or participates, but *not both*.

Discussing the Game Experience

People find the learning experience associated with games more satisfying if play is stopped periodically for group discussions (Chartier, 1972). After each discussion, participants can resume play and try alternate strategies or reinforce concepts learned during the game or in the group discussion. Although the facilitator's manual may suggest how a discussion needs to be handled, the questions depend on the facilitator's purpose.

Although there is no universal way to structure the group discussion, some suggestions may prove helpful. Since simulation games tend to generate a high level of interaction, participants need to discuss what happened during the game and how they feel about it. The facilitator is the key to the quality of the discussion. Participants often like to talk about a game in personal terms—"Who did what to whom?"—before going on to more substantive matters. This aspect of the discussion can be an important experience in gaining insights into interpersonal relationships. Because the interaction between participants is obviously genuine, it gives individuals an opportunity to express how they feel about how they were treated by others during the experience. This discussion should be cordial, and the basic worth of participants should never be questioned.

The facilitator should also lead the group in a discussion of the game model. This discussion gives the participants an opportunity to verbalize their understanding of the general principles underlying the simulation and to question or elaborate on the understanding of the others. During this phase the facilitator may—if appropriate—identify the winning teams or individuals and discuss the winning strategies.

A facilitator can use the participants' experiences in the game as a takeoff point for discussing the reality that has been simulated. This discussion process has at least two training payoffs: (1) It prompts participants to explicate their beliefs about the social reality being simulated and (2) it provides an opportunity for the facilitator to confront participants with alternative ways of viewing the referent reality.

The facilitator should encourage participants to be explicit about their experience with and in the game and to examine this experience in relation to their views of real social systems. A leading question could be "How do you think the game (or some aspect of it) compares with the real world?" If the participants claim the real world is different, then the next logical questions are "How do you think reality is different?" and "Why is reality different?" Other ideas for discussing insights from simulation games can be found in Gaw (1979).

Possible Postgame Activities

One of the fundamental values of games is their ability to stimulate interest and conversation. The creative facilitator will take advantage of this and link it to other training experiences. The opportunities for interlinkage are limited only by a person's own perceptions. Listed below are a few suggestions:

1. After a group has played and discussed a simulation game, it may be motivated to pursue other activities related to the theme. For example, after playing "Dignity" a group may want to visit a ghetto and discuss life in a ghetto with the people who live there.

2. After playing a game the participants may want to change some of the game components or construct a new game. In "Generation Gap," for example, participants may like to change the issues for discussion between the parent and the teenager. They may include issues from their daily conversation or religious values and ideas. The teenagers may want to play it with their own parents.

3. Someone might be assigned to observe and report on the participants' behavior during a game. After playing "Starpower"—which tends to bring out unjust, fascistic, or racist behavior in the squares—a group may become interested in a study of human nature.

DESIGNING SIMULATION GAMES

If a game that fits the training objectives cannot be located, a facilitator may design one. The designing process includes identifying training objectives, describing the social system, structuring the game, and writing the rules.

Identifying Training Objectives. Knowing what needs to be accomplished with a training event is the first step in designing a simulation. The most difficult task is to decide what aspects of a given social system to leave out and which to include. The game will be easier to design if the training objectives are clear, precise, and specific.

Describing the Social System. The social system needs to be selected, carefully analyzed, and described with respect to its systemic components (players, goals and objectives, activities, structure, resources, values, and constraints). The analysis should define the social system by identifying the characteristics of the components, the interlinkages of the elements and their properties, and the operational processes of the diverse units with respect to the whole system.

Structuring the Game. After the conceptual model of a social system has been explicated, the facilitator is ready to develop a simulation game based on these elements. The structuring process involves designing, testing, redesigning, retesting, etc., until the product is satisfactory. The designer should remember that "game design is not only not a science, it is hardly a craft, but rather an 'art' in the sense that we have no explicit rules to transmit" (Boocock & Schild, 1968, p. 266).

The designer begins by creating a rough game format that seeks correpondence between the simulation and a given social reality. Decisions are necessary on the ways that the primary components will interact with each other. As each component is placed in the game its interface with other components needs careful consideration, because the matching of each component with the others will determine the success or failure of the game. The degree of likeness in form between the game components and the social-system components will determine whether or not the participants experience the simulated reality intended.

Writing the Rules. Easily understood game rules are as important as the game structure. According to Livingston and Stoll (1973, p. 30), answers to the following questions will help the participants to understand the rules:

1. What social reality does the game simulate?
2. What is the purpose of the game?

3. What does each of the game materials represent?
4. How is the game set up for playing?
5. What is the order of game play?
6. What do the participants do during each step?
7. How might a participant play a typical round of the game?
8. How does the simulation end?

As the game is put into play, problems will appear that could not be anticipated. It is important to note the successful features of the game design as well as those that failed. In observing the game play, the designer should check for both *playability* and *realism*.

A simulation game is playable if it functions well as a game. Participants must desire to play it, and they must be able to engage themselves in it. It must be interesting, enjoyable, and easily learned. The game must also be manageable.

Realism involves three questions: (1) Does the game accurately represent those aspects of the real-life social system that it is intended to simulate?, (2) Does it include the most critical aspects of the real situation and simulate them in sufficient detail?, and (3) Does it provide a feeling of being in a real social situation? After the prototype has been tested for playability and realism, the necessary adjustments should be made. Each component needs to be examined to determine if changes are required. Then careful attention should be given to rewriting the rules before testing the game again. Although further revisions may be necessary, participants can learn from an unfinished version of a game. Indeed, they may learn as much from suggesting revisions as from playing it in its final form.

CONCLUSION

Simulations are one of the most involving technologies available to the human relations facilitator. Social simulations are based on social systems and potentially can communicate holistic awareness and understandings. Facilitating such games requires careful preparation, skillful administration, and effective discussion. Designing simulation games requires theoretical model building of a social system, constructing a game based on the model, and a process of testing and redesigning.

REFERENCES

Boocock, S.S., & Schild, E.O. (Eds.). (1968). *Simulation games in learning.* Beverly Hills, CA: Sage.

Chartier, M.R. (1972). Learning effect: An experimental study of a simulation game and instrumented discussion. *Simulation & Games, 3,* 203-218.

Chartier, M.R. (1973). *Simulation games as learning devices: A summary of empirical findings and their implication for the utilization of games in instruction.* Covina, CA: American Baptist Seminary of the West. (ERIC Document Reproduction Service No. ED 101 384).

Gaw, B.A. (1979). Processing questions: An aid to completing the learning cycle. In J.E. Jones & J.W. Pfeiffer (Eds.), *The 1979 annual handbook for group facilitators.* San Diego, CA: University Associates.

Greenblat, C.S. (1975). From theory to model to gaming-simulation: A case study and validity test. In C.S. Greenblat & R.D. Duke (Eds.), *Gaming-simulation: Rationale, design, and applications.* New York: Halsted Press.

Hall, A.D., & Fagen, R.E. (1975). Definition of system. In B.D. Ruben & J.Y. Kim (Eds.), *General systems theory and human communication.* Rochelle Park, NJ: Hayden Book.

Horn, R.E., & Cleaves, A. (Eds.). (1980). *The guide to simulations/games for education and training* (4th ed.). Beverly Hills, CA: Sage.

Jones, J.E., & Pfeiffer, J.W. (1975). Introduction to the theory and practice section. In J.E. Jones & J.W. Pfeiffer (Eds.), *The 1975 annual handbook for group facilitators.* San Diego, CA: University Associates.

Katz, D., & Kahn, R.L. (1978). *The social psychology of organizations* (2nd ed.). New York: John Wiley.

Livingston, S.A., & Stoll, C.S. (1973). *Simulation games: An introduction for the social studies teacher.* New York: The Free Press.

Olsen, M.E. (1968). *The process of social organization.* New York: Holt, Rinehart and Winston.

Appendix 2:
Additional Resources for
Simulation Games

Many sources for simulations and games are listed in the *References and Bibliography* preceding Appendix 1. The following are additional sources that may be helpful.

Professional Associations

North American Simulation and Gaming Association
University of North Carolina at Asheville
One University Heights
Asheville, North Carolina 28804-3299
(704) 251-6023
Executive Director: Dr. Bahram Farzanegan

NASAGA promotes information and the exchange of ideas with game designers in North America and from around the world. Membership benefits include a subscription to SIMAGES (a quarterly newsletter) and the Sage publication *Simulation and Games.* Several games published by the national headquarters are available to members at a discount, and members have access to the national archives. NASAGA also holds an annual conference. Membership fee is $50/year.

International Simulation and Gaming Association
NASAGA Representative: Richard D. Duke
MULTILOGUE/Richard D. Duke & Associates, Inc.
321 Parklake
Ann Arbor, Michigan 48103
(313) 663-3690

General Secretary: Prof. Dr. Jan Klabbers
c/o Faculty of Sciences
P.O. Box 80140
3508 TC Utrecht
The Netherlands

ISAGA seeks to further the development, application, and use of simulation and gaming materials throughout the world. Facilitates communication between scholars and practitioners, promotes training in the field, promotes the development of better methods, and encourages the formation of national and regional groups. Membership benefits include four newsletters per year and reductions in fees for conferences, workshops, seminars, etc., in which ISAGA participates. ISAGA has adopted the journal *Simulations and Games*, published by Sage. It also organizes annual conferences, each in a different location around the world.

Periodicals

Simages **Newsletter**
Included with NASAGA membership.
Contact Katherine, NASAGA Secretary, at address given above.

Simulations and Games: An International Journal of Theory, Design and Research
Sage Publications, Inc.
275 South Beverly Drive
Beverly Hills, California 90212

(Subscription rate: $32/year, $96/three years, $9/issue. Subscription included with NASAGA membership.)